THE QUICK WHITE PAPER

Sherman N. Miller

S.N. Miller of Delaware, Ltd.

Second Printing August 1999.

Published by S.N.M. Publishing Company (a division of S.N. Miller of Delaware, Ltd.), 2006 N. Van Buren Street, Wilmington, DE 19802-3808, **www.snmiller.com.**

Production assistance provided by Michele Jones, Electro Galley, 24 Hayward Drive, Surry, NH 03431.

Copyright © 1996 by Sherman N. Miller. All rights reserved. No part of this publication may be reproduced, transmitted, transcribed, stored in a retrieval system, or translated into any language in any form by any means without written permission.

ISBN 0-9640915-3-4 $19.95 (U.S.)

Library of Congress: TXu 723-498

THE QUICK WHITE PAPER

DEDICATION

To my wife of thirty-five years, **_Gwynelle W. Miller_**. She has been my faithful editor of over 500 newspaper editorials, numerous letters to the editor, articles for magazines and trade publications, and so on. I greatly appreciate her candid opinions in our discussions of various works.

ACKNOWLEDGMENTS

The author wishes to express great appreciation to Mr. Francis Joyce, Chief Editorial Consultant of S.N.M. Publishing Company; Ms. Ruth Wilson, Instructor in Office Systems at Delaware Technical and Community College; Dr. Edward H. Kerner, Professor of Physics at the University of Delaware; Mr. Edwin M. Stephenson (retired DuPont Company Technical Marketing Associate); Mr. Leo de Vos, Former Technical Account Manager Akzo Nobel in The Netherlands; and Ms. Mary Moy, Former Manager of Center for Career Excellence at MBNA bank, for their editorial comments on this work.

A thank you to Mr. James E. Leary for designing the cover of this volume, to Mr. Bernard Pearce of Delaware Technical and Community College Marketing Department for designing the Web-book cover, and to Marge Painter (retired DuPont Company Graphic Artist) for designing the table of contents template.

A special thank you to Ms. Sammye Elizabeth Miller II, a Mechanical Engineering student at Cornell University, for her contributions to technical papers employed in this book and for developing our Website.

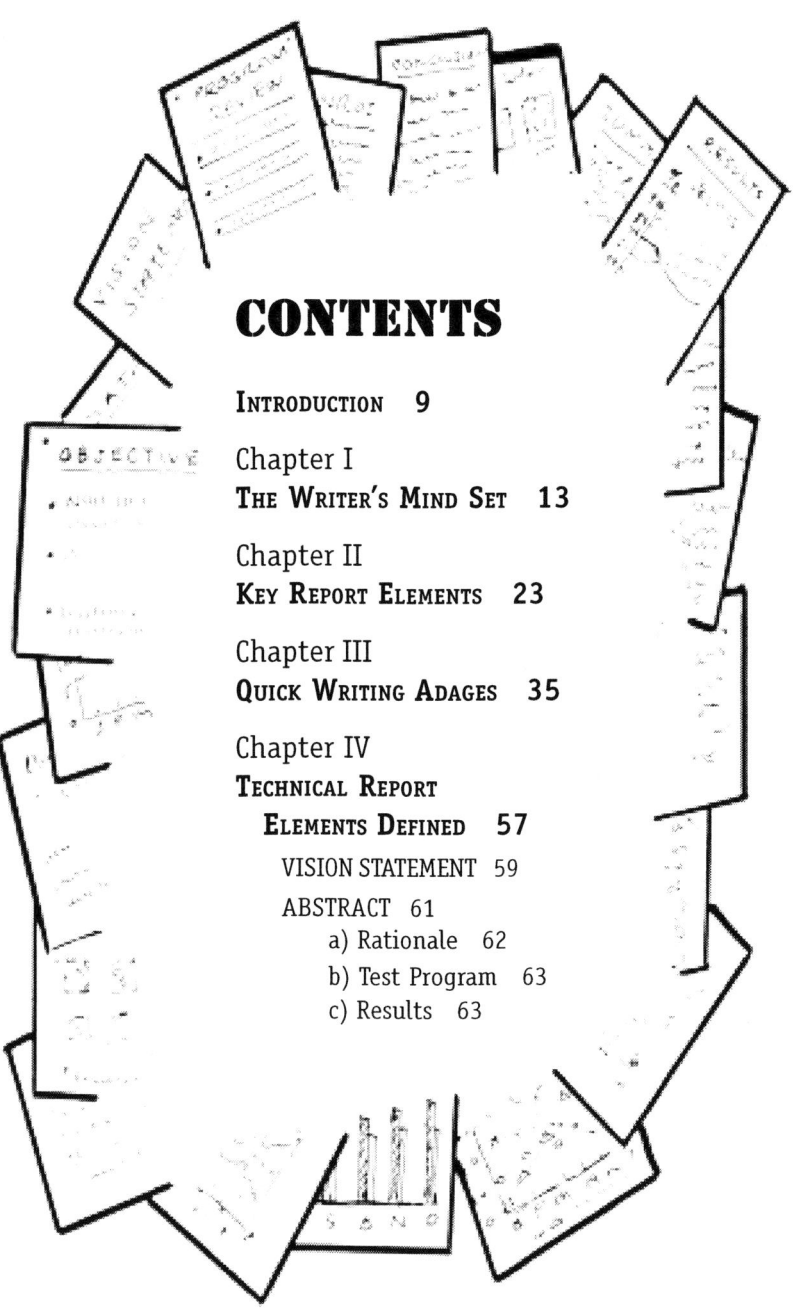

CONTENTS

INTRODUCTION 9

Chapter I
THE WRITER'S MIND SET 13

Chapter II
KEY REPORT ELEMENTS 23

Chapter III
QUICK WRITING ADAGES 35

Chapter IV
TECHNICAL REPORT ELEMENTS DEFINED 57

   VISION STATEMENT 59

   ABSTRACT 61
     a) Rationale 62
     b) Test Program 63
     c) Results 63

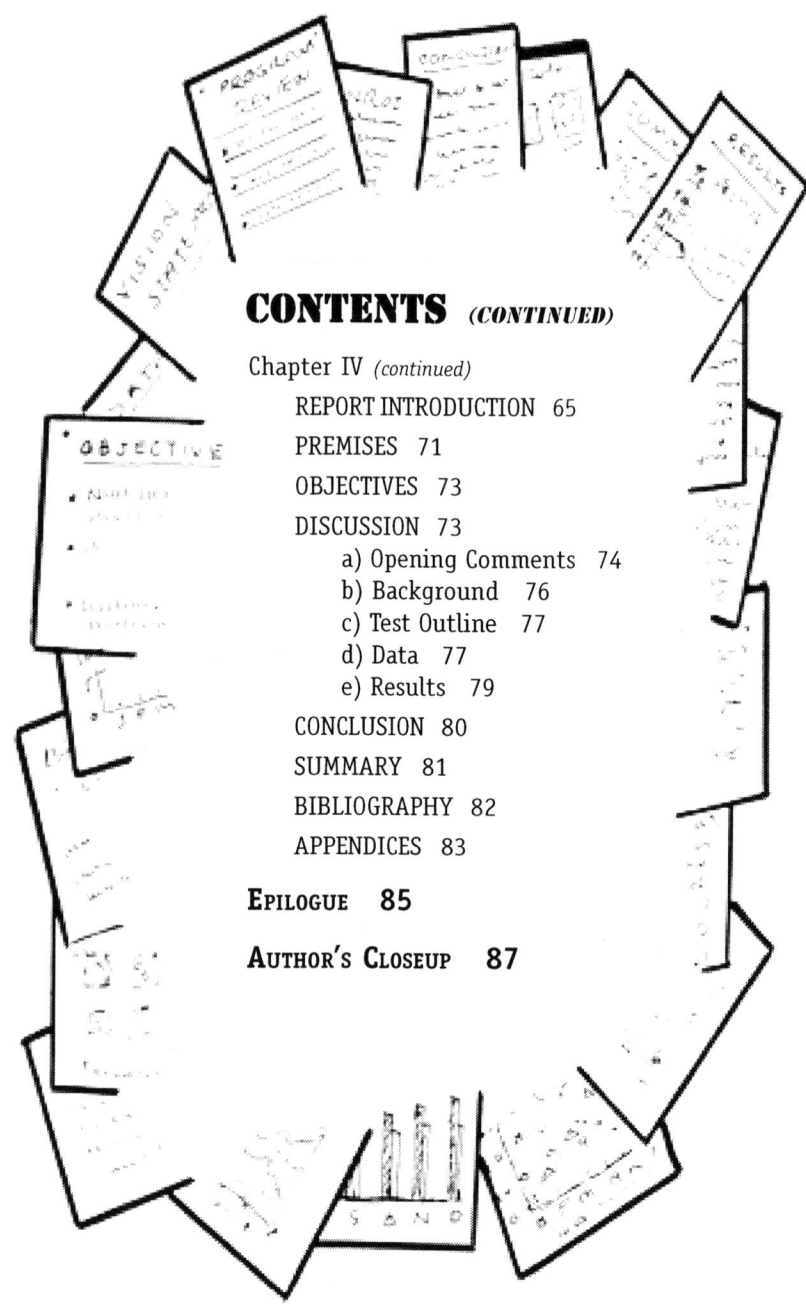

CONTENTS *(CONTINUED)*

Chapter IV *(continued)*
    REPORT INTRODUCTION 65
    PREMISES 71
    OBJECTIVES 73
    DISCUSSION 73
        a) Opening Comments 74
        b) Background 76
        c) Test Outline 77
        d) Data 77
        e) Results 79
    CONCLUSION 80
    SUMMARY 81
    BIBLIOGRAPHY 82
    APPENDICES 83

EPILOGUE 85

AUTHOR'S CLOSEUP 87

INTRODUCTION

A common scene at industrial conferences is to hear the moderator plead for people to volunteer to deliver trade or technical papers at the next meeting. There is always a sudden chill in the air while everyone wonders who the new "volunteers" will be. In some cases, bosses volunteer their subordinates when it looks like a key business objective can be accomplished with a trade paper or when failure to present something brings doubt on the corporation's commitment to this market. In any event, one does not see people aggressively pursuing the opportunity to present papers.

This ritual suggests that writing and presenting a technical paper is something that takes too much valuable time for too little return on investment. Some might argue, "In academia it is publish or perish, but in industry it is patent or perish." Furthermore, you have to undergo a grueling process to get something approved for presentation in industry. When the above statements are overlaid with scientists' comments over the years such as, "I can do the research, but I can't write it up," it is very disquieting for the future competitiveness of American business in the global marketplace.

The Quick White Paper

This disquietude is heightened as you listen to the disdain in the voices of retired scientists railing over the general inability of today's young scientists to write coherent sentences using proper words. "I had a young fellow send me something with the word professor spelled p-r-o-f-e-s-s-e-r," complained a school board member. Another retired scientist pointed out that modern young scientists and engineers don't know the difference between *their* and *there* in writing a sentence. The tragedy here is that these chaps feel that the school system perpetuates this problem, for they contend that school papers are examined for content and not grammar.

Although these concerns over poor grammar are alarming, the problem is not as critical as it might have been thirty years ago. Modern high-calibre word processing software, such as *WordPerfect* and *Microsoft Word*, include both grammar and spelling checkers. The proper use of these tools allows a writer to significantly reduce grammar and spelling problems with human editors polishing the rest. Also the commercialization of speech recognition programs, such as *Via Voice Gold* by International Business Machines, portends to allow you to avoid hours of tedious typing by permitting you to dictate your ideas directly into your word processing program.

Thus, the real problem is: Many corporate scientists and engineers spend years doing research without formally reporting their findings in a manner that is retrievable by future generations. Some scientists and engineers become quite adept at finding ways of not reporting their findings in formal, internal, technical reports, by writing letters to their boss summarizing their work. These letters are great for their current management, but may get lost in the file-purging of future bosses. When the company attempts to resurrect dormant projects, new hires find themselves initiating completely new efforts without any knowledge of what happened in the past. This is a terrible waste of corporate resources. We are reinventing the wheel because we lost the blueprint.

Introduction

Other scientists are convinced that their laboratory notes are sufficient documentation of their efforts. The research notebook is excellent for keeping detailed records of scientists' and engineers' work, protecting these efforts in a court of law. Many scientists and engineers do a good job of indexing these notebooks, so if you can find the right notebook, you can get all the details you want on their research effort. However, one may be more interested in conclusions than poring through page after page of research findings. Therefore, the research notebook is excellent for recording the day-to-day scientific efforts, but it may fall short of providing quick conclusions from corporate research.

Today, many corporations are recreating the wheel about every seven years as a result of new employees not knowing the results from earlier efforts. Early and forced retirements (as many corporations rationalized operations in the 1990s to improve their productivity) widened the knowledge gap between corporate scientific generations. There are few people left that a young scientist or engineer can ask, "Did anyone ever do something like this before and what happened?" This is a serious waste of corporate intellectual property, for new market opportunities or strategic direction shifts may exist in research now laying dormant in research notebooks. The exodus of many senior scientists and engineers has created a need to make corporate intellectual property more accessible to young personnel. Ignorance of the past is very expensive and a waste of corporate resources.

There is a school of thought which says that, "If you are attacking tomorrow's problems with today's solutions, you should not be surprised when you are displaced in the marketplace by a superior product." Good research and development: in-house or bought through acquisition is the only insurance against obsolescence. Corporations need to know what discoveries they have in their arsenal if this intellectual property is to be useful in fostering their growth and continuing their long term profitability. But today's lean organization, where everyone must wear many hats, forces everyone to prioritize their projects, subordinating long-term needs to short-term gains. In this environment, many scientists and engineers look upon writing technical reports as a chore instead of an opportunity to have their efforts guarantee the long term viability of the corporation.

A little forethought when recording one's research findings will make reporting on your efforts quicker and less painful. This book will introduce methods to write multiple reports — an internal technical paper, an internal technical presentation, an external trade presentation and a technical trade publication — *all at the same time*.

We assume that modern scientists and engineers have some degree of proficiency with word processing, spreadsheet, and graphics programs in order to take full advantage of the ideas and suggestions we offer.

Chapter I

THE WRITER'S MIND SET

In the first step in our journey to learn to write technical reports and papers quickly, we use the model of the new writer trying to overcome writer's block as a guide to conquering our own technical writing procrastination. We shall view technical writing as no more difficult than other writing forms. We will see technical authors experiencing similar writing problems to their colleagues. Through the eyes of a writer overwhelmed by writer's obstacles, we will glean some ideas on how scientists and engineers can overcome writing gridlock.

Imagine getting up Saturday morning, dashing out of your house and hopping into your car for a spin. The next thing you know you are zipping down the expressway without a care in the world, enchanted by beautiful music filling your ears. Being a task-oriented person, roughly a half hour later you ask yourself, "Where am I going?"

The Quick White Paper

You abhor wasting time. The first thought that pops into your mind is, "Do I turn around?" This is followed by another disquieting question, "Do I pull off the road until I can really decide what to do?" Before your nerves calm down, you are whispering to yourself, "I'll await some divine revelation, then I'll know what to do."

Your previous joy is now a headache because turning around means you've wasted your time, money for gasoline, and the wear and tear on your automobile. James Wilmore, Fire Chief of the City of Wilmington, Delaware, has a proverb that describes your decision-making dilemma. "You get nothing for starting and stopping."

Your stress heightens as you realize the foolhardiness in continuing to drive aimlessly without a goal, for it means that you are going nowhere fast. You are a person who likes to control his or her own destiny; thus, you are perturbed that your well-being is now in the hands of fate. Instinctively, you know that counting on luck is only for professional gamblers. Ordinary people are discomfited by the idea of "luck."

Having writer's block is like driving a car without a travel plan. Picture a person staring into a huge, blank, computer screen with bloodshot eyes ... fingers locked in a writing position ... writer's block! Yet this nightmare, this Herculean task need not become self-defeating if you get your mind set in the proper order for writing. Using the driving scenario, let us develop the proper mind set for writing good, internal reports and publishable papers that are user-friendly.

We hear many excuses for people not writing reports and articles. An industrial research scientist provided a classic: "Trade journal articles are a real labor of love." You hear phrases like, "I love to write literature but not that boring technical stuff." Still others contend, "That literary stuff is just too emotional for me to waste my time on. I need to get to the point and not waste a lot of time describing the sky as blue and the trees green."

Pulling off the road to plan your journey is comparable to the first basic principle of good writing. *Have a clear mind to capture your emotions, because pens, pencils, word processors, and typewriters are mere tools for putting your thoughts into words.*

In learning to write newspaper articles, this writer rewrote his first effort eleven times before something of publishing calibre emerged. Asked to look at the first draft, my wife Gwynelle commented, "It is the worst thing I have ever read."

Her words were a crushing blow to my ego and engendered an "I'll show you" attitude. But in the final analysis Gwynelle was right. My draft lacked coherent thinking and merely rambled over some vague issue.

Driven solely by pride to regain my stature in Gwynelle's eyes, I rewrote the article again and again repeating, however, the same mistakes. After nine rewrites my nerves calmed and my mind opened. It was clear that I needed to think before attempting to write, so a five mile walk seemed the perfect thing to do. During this walk my thoughts became clear, and I could see the issue as plain as day. Once it was clear what I was going to write about, it took only two drafts to get something publishable: one draft to record my emotion and another draft to clean up the grammar. I later got paid for this work.

This learning experience guided my writing on over 500 newspaper editorials, many technical and trade reports, technical presentations, technical and business articles, and manuals during my career to date. It made me prolific enough to write seven internal technical reports, three technical articles and presentations for business societies, and roughly forty newspaper editorials in 1993, the year I retired from the Du Pont Company as a Technical Marketing Specialist. Thus, my varied writing experiences have taught me that the basis of quick writing is, *"Five minutes worth of thinking is worth five hours of writing."*

No one is surprised to hear research scientists and engineers say, "Just give me the data and I'm happy, but don't ask me to write it up. It takes me forever to get something written." These statements can mean career suicide for some corporate scientists and engineers because they are in a "publish or perish" job when it comes to upward mobility.

If technocrats think clearly about the one emotion they want their intended audience to take from their article, report, or presentation, they will not find writing an overwhelming experience. Remember that writing with unclarified ideas is like asking your audience to build a puzzle without any idea of the shape of the pieces or their color scheme. Don't be intimidated by a blank computer screen begging your fingers to do something. Forethought can mentally write the first, second, and third draft of your work, placing you on the path to producing an excellent publication or a very convincing story in short order.

Forethought is sometimes discarded with the excuse that "I know what I want to say, but I just can't seem to say it." A holistic look at this comment suggests that we really don't know what we want to say, and have refused to ponder the subject long enough to arrive at what needs to be presented. Or we are nervous that others will exploit our efforts against us. We may not have considered to whom the work is directed. We may not be sure of our overt and covert agendas in doing this work. We may be afraid to write up our technical work for it will highlight the holes in our research. We may feel that others will take our job once they understand our research findings and no longer need us.

We can learn something from historical figures that will help us overcome this quagmire. Dr. Martin Luther King, Jr. is an excellent example of a leader who possessed a clear picture of what he thought tomorrow should look like. He made that clear in his famous *I Have A Dream* speech, suggesting that he wanted to see a world where people are judged by their character and not the color of their skin.

President Franklin Roosevelt believed that government could help people. He used government to help millions of people to a better life. They understood his dream, and he is probably as close to a king as one could get for a U.S. President. My late father's understanding of Roosevelt's vision rings clear in my mind even today as I recall my dad declaring, "Roosevelt was for the working man."

When you look at the key traits of the above leaders, you quickly notice that good ones know that *in order to shape tomorrow's world, you must first have a vision today of what you want tomorrow to look like.* Writers are leaders through their works; thus a vision of the future is the first mental draft of your work. You must spend whatever time is necessary to carefully determine how you visualize tomorrow when your work is published. Everything else in the external or internal publication hinges on the quality of your vision.

A good *vision statement* is a key element in rapid writing for technical and newspaper articles, newsletters, and books. This statement gives meaning to your work by providing you with a holistic assessment of your data that permits you to produce a consistent story that the audience can understand. It is also necessary if you want your work to be user-friendly, *for it reduces the writing fog factor by shifting the emphasis to writing an understandable document versus one which merely impresses a handful of peers.* In the corporate world, it is better to have mass understanding of your work, for you significantly enhance the chances of it being used and of you being rewarded.

Vision statements address key issues. They answer such questions as: Will your article or book make obsolete an existing theory? Are you telling your peers that you have developed an improved or new product or clarified scientific understanding? Do you want to merely show off your expertise in a given area?

Establishing your vision statement and clarifying issues is the business of your first draft. This is very critical for further writing efforts. Not doing this job well will lead to many frustrating moments and difficulty in writing.

In writing the second draft in your mind, you want to begin to answer the questions posed in the vision statement of your first draft. Here is where you must separate fact from fantasy. *Trying to do too much in one report will make it very confusing and difficult to write.* Therefore, if you have multiple issues in your vision statement, perhaps you should rethink it. A good vision statement is nothing more than a holistic idea of what you want the outcome of your report to be. It is usually best if one single, unifying thought makes up this statement.

In your third mental draft, start addressing tactical issues that get the writing process underway. Here is another series of questions that need mental answers and stimulate writing: "Am I trying to sell my ideas in the mass market where people will get bored quickly if things are not explained simply? What are the core findings of my work and how do I wish to present them to senior management? Do I have access to the data I need to make my case? Did my data come from credible sources and sound research?"

In this third mental draft, you also start to overlay your vision with the amount of resources you have to make the final result a reality. This can be a gut-wrenching process, because an honest assessment of your paper's publishing potential (for both your corporation's staff and for outside publications that can evolve from this work) is a necessary condition for expending your time on it, unless of course you are doing research for your own gratification. You must ask yourself, *"Does anyone really care what I have to say, and if they do, what piques their interest?"*

If you get trapped in the chasm between fact and fantasy, you will find out that publishers have no problem letting you know that your work does not meet their needs. Your immediate management will do likewise when it comes to giving you a poor annual performance rating for wasting their time on reading your balderdash.

You are now ready to write mental draft number four. The cost of obtaining credible data now stares you in the face if you do not already have it. If you conclude that the cost/benefit for the data is too great, you should terminate your plans before you waste valuable time and money. On the other hand, *having done your self-analysis, you are in a strong position to place your efforts before management, if that becomes necessary.* Management has a limited budget from whence to operate and a strong case gives you a leg up in getting their support for your project.

The fourth mental draft also gives you an opportunity to re-ask, "Who really is my audience? What data do I really need to make my case? *Can I write my vision statement down in less than three sentences (preferably one sentence)?"*

A clear vision statement is the cornerstone of rapid writing and its refinement gets you through the first four drafts of your work. Time spent perfecting your vision statement will pay large dividends in making your work successful.

You also want to remember that technical writing puts your credibility on the line, so you should give prior thought to your actions. Forethought is well worth the time invested in it. One is reminded how user-unfriendly personal computer equipment and software manuals are and how few people waste their time plowing through this material. These manuals are classic examples of engineers writing to other engineers but trying to pretend that they can be used in a mass market of computer users who do not have engineering, mathematics, or science backgrounds. Software companies are now paying the price for this high engineering fog factor by working with

The Quick White Paper

large technical support organizations in order to continue growing in the consumer market.

Some software companies, however, have seen the light. To economically offer software in the mass market, they had to make user-friendliness a priority rather than merely a buzz word. They simply cannot afford huge staffs of engineers to answer customer questions.

Today computers are in roughly one third of America's homes where "user-friendly" is the operative phrase. There is no doubt that the growth in the home computer market will follow the lead of the telephone and television. Thus, *the thought of user-friendliness will be pervasive in the national and international psyche in the not too distant future.*

Brainstorming over.

Now, *and only now,*
are you ready to begin to write!

Chapter II

KEY REPORT ELEMENTS

When attempting to write quickly, a presupposition is that you have a crystal clear picture in your mind of what you intend to say. Additionally, there are four key tools a writer must have to write technical reports and articles quickly. They are a clear vision statement, a set of premises, the test measurements or theoretical calculations, and a personal computer or a workstation. The computer should have high calibre word processing, spreadsheet, and graphic software capability.

A detailed discussion of each of these items will follow; however, we offer some working definitions here to maintain clarity:

Vision Statement is the picture in your mind of the outcome of your report, such as increased sales volume, increased earnings, and so on.

The Quick White Paper

Premises are the ground rules to view your data when it comes time to analyze it. They are things you assume to be true although you may find later from your data that they need refining or are simply not true and must be discarded.

Data are the experimental measurements or theoretical calculations that fuel the report.

Computer is the personal computer, workstation, or mainframe terminal that offers word processing, graphics, and spreadsheet capability.

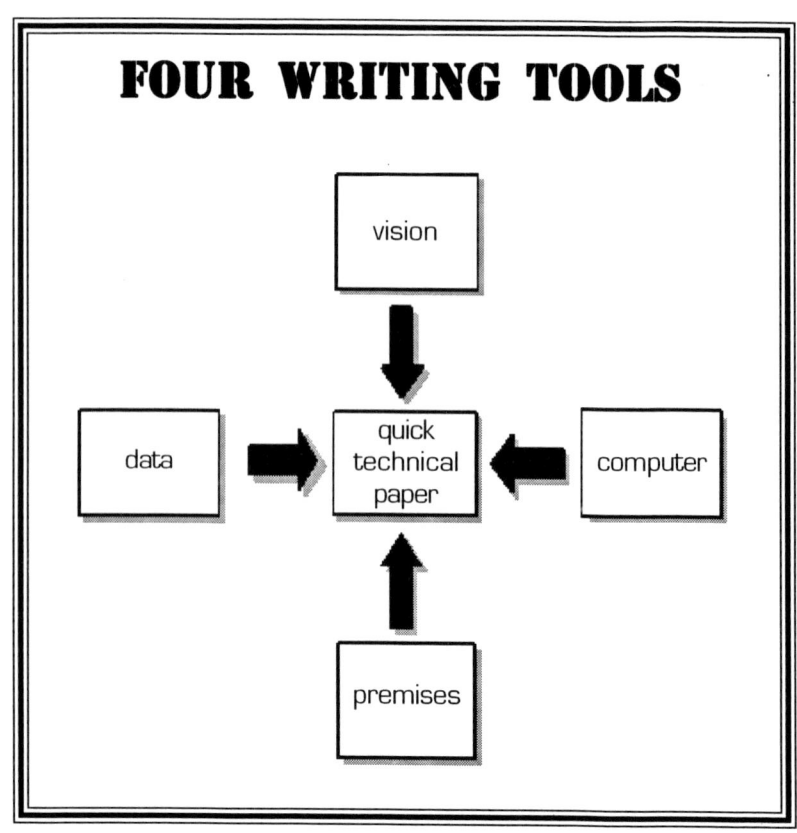

Key Report Elements

These four writing tools are the means to developing your technical report. We cannot overemphasize the importance of having each item, as they will assist you to avoid getting bogged down in a quagmire of confusion.

We are now ready to use a technical report writing template to get the writing effort underway. We offer the following elements for a technical report. This report will be one that can easily evolve into a trade publication or an internal publication and presentation.

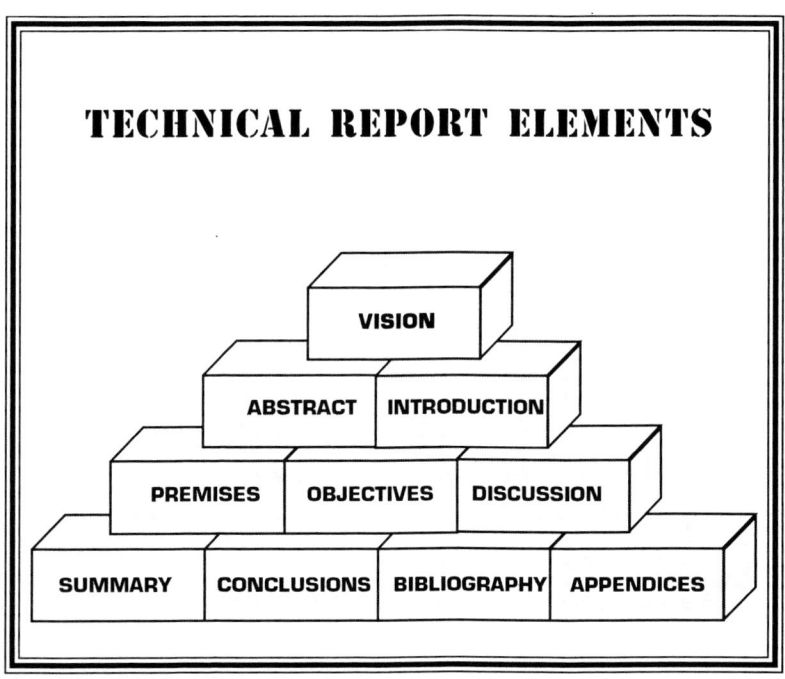

The ability to write several reports simultaneously using this template hinges on clearly writing each of the above elements in such a way that their non-confidential portions are portable to new instruments, and that all tables, charts and graphs have conclusions written on them whenever appropriate.

The Quick White Paper

If, for example, you want to write a research paper from an internal technical report, you merely need to remove the confidential information from this existing work and you have a large portion of your work done. You can readily see this technique when comparing a trade publication to the original technical report; both contain similar elements.

FIGURE I

TABLE I

FILAMENT ANALYSIS

KINK BANDS:

HEAVY = 500+   MEDIUM = 250+   LIGHT = 100-

VERY LIGHT = 25-   VERY VERY LIGHT = 5-

SAMPLE	#	KINK BANDS	FIBRILLATION	SPLIT	CRUSHED ENDS
TEST	1	390	20	0	4
ITEM	2	250	20	1	6
	3	178	21	1	2
	4	255	20	0	2
	5	112	21	0	1

* HIGH FIBRILLATION SUGGESTS CORD ABRASION

* CRUSHED ENDS REDUCE CORD STRENGTH

* MODERATE KINK BANDS INDICATE AXIAL COMPRESSION OR BENDING OF FILAMENTS

Key Report Elements

We need to examine examples of charts, graphs, and tables to fully appreciate the issue of *data portability*. First, let us look at Figure I, originally published as Table I in the technical paper, "Systematic Techniques of Hose Failure Mode Analysis," 910577 in the Society of Automotive Engineers (SAE) Technical Paper Series.

It contains a principal rating system for the key data displayed, namely kink bands. It has summaries of several observations, and ends with conclusions stating what the data indicates. These details allow the author to easily turn Table I into a slide or transparency for a presentation to technical management. However, its level of detail may be too high to make it interesting to pure marketing or sales management.

FIGURE II

TABLE V
CALCULATIONS VERSUS EXPERIMENTAL FINDINGS

CORD CONSTRUCTION DENIER/TYPE	TECHNIQUE TYPE	BURST PRESSURE (BAR)	CORD LENGTH PER HOSE PITCH (MM)	CORD WEIGHT PER 50.8 mm HOSE LENGTH (GRAMS)
1200/2 MPD-T	ACTUAL	20.3	153	0.696
1200/2 MPD-T	CALCULATED	21.2	151	0.644
1500/1 PPD/POP-T	ACTUAL	28.1	154	0.400
1500/1 PPD/POP-T	CALCULATED	27.5	150	0.399
1500/1 PPD-T	ACTUAL	29.2	158	0.404
1500/1 PPD-T	CALCULATED	30.4	150	0.399

* CALCULATED VALUES PREDICT EXPERIMENTAL FINDINGS

The Quick White Paper

Figure II, orginally published as Table V from #930151 of SAE Technical Paper Series, offers a look at a technical chart that is very attractive to marketing and sales management. It points out that a theoretical method for calculating knit hose burst pressure and the weight of reinforcement per unit length of hose has been developed. This allows one to do paper studies and develop optimum cost/benefit without the need to build hoses.

Sales engineers also can use these equations to negotiate value-in-use pricing with customers and guide them on the proper reinforcement type to use in a given application. Questions such as, "Is it better to use a quantity of a weak inexpensive reinforcement material or an expensive, light weight, high-strength cord?" now can be debated by sales engineers equipped with the means to assess the value of various products to the customer.

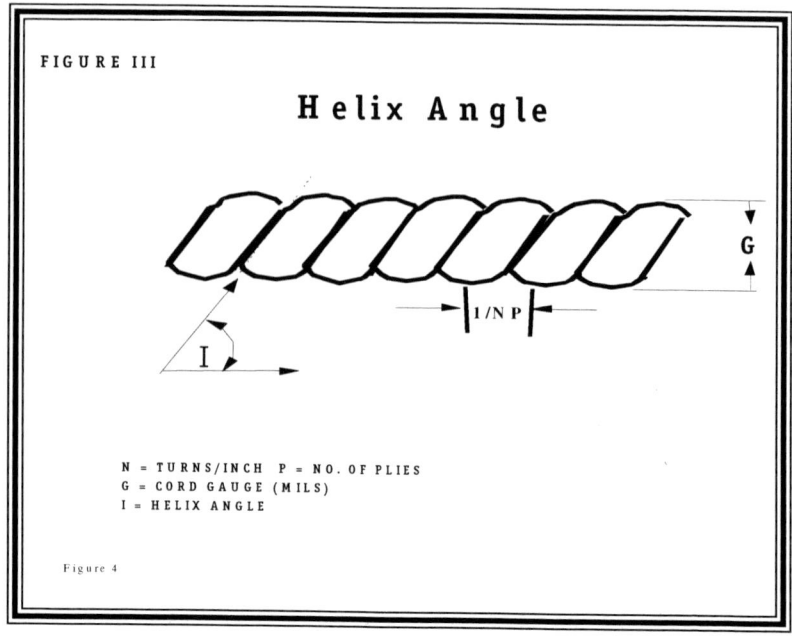

Figure 4

Key Report Elements

Continuing this portability discussion, we now turn to charts. There are basically two types. The first family of charts are those that help you to understand the science of an issue; they do not lend themselves to having conclusions written on them. The second family of charts are those with conclusions to your research; they may be of greater interest to non-technical personnel such as strategic planners, marketers and the sales force that use your findings to enhance the growth of business.

Figure III entitled, "HELIX ANGLE" helps to paint a clear picture of the parameters of low twist versus high twist yarn and cord. It first appeared as Figure 4 in the technical paper entitled, "Knitted Heater Hose Static Equations: Burst Pressure and Economics," presented to the International Society of Industrial Fabric Manufacturers Fall Conference in 1993.

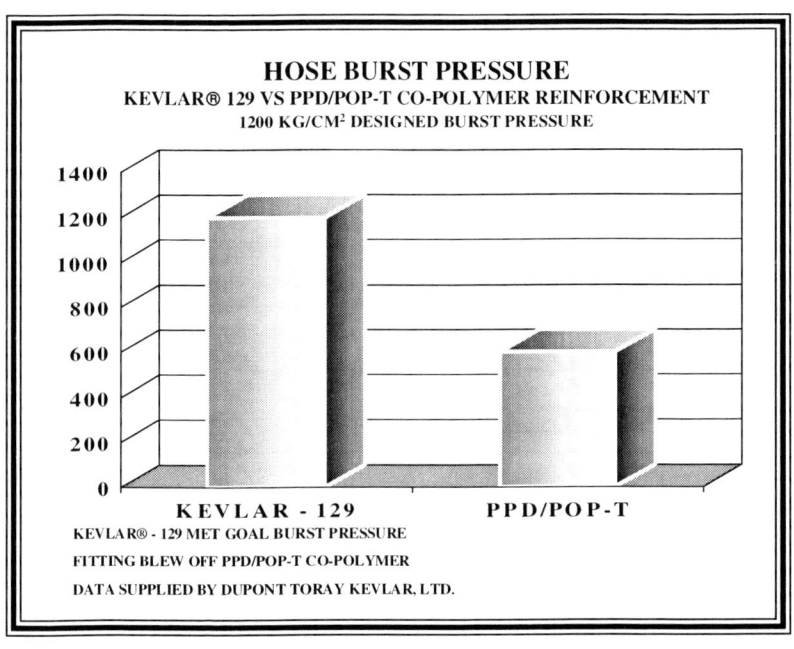

The ability of marketing to use technical findings in papers to bolster a perceived competitive product superiority in the global marketplace is evident in Figure IV, first presented as Figure 10 in the technical paper entitled, "Aramid Transverse Filament Properties And Hose Fitting Retention." This is a joint effort of Sherman N. Miller and Warren F. Knoff. It was presented in March 1993 to the Detroit Rubber Group a subdivision of the Rubber Division of the American Chemical Society.

The marketing value of this chart becomes obvious as we look at the comments in the technical paper accompanying it: "The above results offer an explanation to findings reported by DuPont Toray Kevlar to an experiment with high pressure hoses reinforced with either KEVLAR® or PPD/POP-T commercial copolymer. The design burst pressure of these hoses is 1200 kg/cm^2 (roughly 17.4 kpsi). Figure 10 shows that the PPD/POP-T copolymer hose failed prematurely and the KEVLAR® 129 achieved the hose burst pressure goal. A blown off fitting was the premature failure mode. A similar experience has also been reported in the United States of America."

You can also see this figure might evolve into a chart for a trade presentation or an internal management review. It shows to senior management in the corporation that a significant chink in the armor of a world class competitor was identified and that business, once perceived at high risk, is less vulnerable than initially thought.

When you start to fully utilize the concept of data portability, there are some common sense items you will want to keep in mind. They are:

1) Remove references that imply your strategic or tactical directions in the present and future.

Key Report Elements

2) Scale your graphs vaguely in such a manner as to avoid burdening the reader with numbers when trends will make your points.

3) Keep in mind that giving out specific recipes for various processes, even though you hold a patent on them, may permit unscrupulous people to simply steal your ideas and reproduce them.

4) Remember that portability depends on the power of the software on your computer. The most powerful versions of spreadsheets, word processors, and graphic programs are your best bet. This present work is being written using *WordPerfect, Lotus 123*, and *Freelance Graphics* running under the Windows operating system.

5) Computers running either the *Microsoft Windows* or *Macintosh* operating systems allow you to easily cut-and-paste information from one program to another or within several open documents in a single program. The makers of these operating systems are continually updating their products to make them even more user friendly.

6) Selecting good software is like selecting a spouse: Once you find one that is suitable, it becomes difficult to make a switch, for you face a high learning curve if you do. If you are spending all of your time learning new software, you do not have time to do useful work. Thus, select your initial software based on its ability to accomplish your tasks, and take solace in the fact that major software companies offer comparable features in their products.

The Quick White Paper

<u>Imagine</u>. . . . You are at a crucial point in research concerning a new or improved product. The Research and Development manager has read your technical report and asks <u>you</u> to make a presentation to the vice president of marketing. Under the old method of preparing technical reports you might have panicked. But now, you stop a minute and think about what a marketing person needs to know about your findings and their potential impact on the business both from the standpoint of competitive advantage as well as simply keeping your product line from becoming obsolete.

You call up your technical report on your computer, and generate a new report that is based largely on portions of the introduction, objectives, summary, and conclusions.

When you develop this presentation, you keep in mind that the marketing people will not be interested in all the minute details of your beautiful research. They are looking for things that indicate a superior product or offer new directions in the marketplace. Thus, *the business rationale you put into your introductory statement should become the driving force of this presentation.*

We will discuss the introduction section a bit more later on, but suffice it to say that it is the place where one justifies to top management the expenditure of corporate funds and its impact on the bottom line. It is very important to keep in mind that you are generating reports for business and not merely satisfying academic curiosity; therefore, you should always keep the business significance of your research effort in front of you. Having a business sense for one's efforts makes their integration into the corporate effort a great deal easier.

You discover how simple it is to merely extract a portion of your master report to meet an immediate need. Of course, you need to do some mild editing or create one-line statements from information reported in paragraph form.

If you take extra effort to write your company technical report carefully, many variations from it, such as targeting a host of audiences, can evolve very quickly. This generation of new reports merely becomes a withdrawal from the storehouse, dependent upon how well one learns to use word processing, spreadsheet, and graphic programs.

Chapter III

QUICK WRITING ADAGES

As we develop our writing skills, we learn to call upon some rules-of-thumb to aid in discovering our own personal writing style. You will no doubt get many words of wisdom on writing from many people. We garnered our share of this advice over the years, and we generated a few ourselves that were the fallout of our own writing efforts. Some adages and ideas that we found to be excellent in getting in the right frame of mind to produce high calibre publications and charts for senior management reviews are discussed in this chapter.

Use only those adages that make sense to you as writing aids, though it may be helpful if you at least try others on for size before you discard them. You want to avoid prematurely ignoring ideas that may help improve your writing productivity. Perhaps you can develop a series of these adages to meet your own personal writing needs as your writing proficiency improves.

The Quick White Paper

Five minutes worth of thinking is worth five hours of writing.

    All writing first takes place in your mind. You want to build a mental hologram of how you want things to be when your work is published and presented. This mental hologram becomes the blueprint from which you develop your project and the framework which allows you to easily prioritize the data you collect during your research effort. Thus, your brain is clearly the most important central processing unit for any data you generate or locate. If you do not have an idea of where you are heading with your data, you will spend hours staring at your blank computer screen hoping for some divine revelation that may never come.

    The short time it takes to think through your goal will pay you back tenfold in your writing efforts, for now you know what information is important and what to discard. Your writing effort has focus. It is tantamount to your addressing a problem like a high powered rifle projectile hitting a target with a great impact at a far distance.

The brain is like other muscles, and it hurts when you first start to use it; but it gets keener with regular exercise, making the mind perform at extraordinary levels.

The brain offers directions to our efforts and everything else is merely a tool to clarify the vision in our minds. It is common knowledge that the development and use of our own brain is paramount to our upward mobility in the economic mainstream. Yet it is often forgotten that developing the brain can be a painful process and may be ignored by many people when it comes to learning to write.

The use of your brain is paramount in assessing any data you generate. Unless you have an idea of what you are seeking, all of the data in the world will be useless to you. You must understand thoroughly what you want to communicate, or you will find yourself merely wasting time staring at your blank computer screen or scribbling on a note pad with little to show for your effort.

The modern engineer or scientist cannot afford to be like an ill-prepared minister I once encountered on a community-based television show. I asked this chap if he prepared his sermons before he went onto the air, for I had no idea what he was saying during the telecast. He replied, "I just let the spirit hit me when I'm on the air." His response left me perplexed, for I had been taught that ministers were to go and teach all nations, and that meant one had to prepare his or her sermons. Clearly you must be willing to put quality work into forming your ideas and not sit haplessly awaiting a divine revelation.

You want to discover all of those activities that are catalysts to *your* thinking process; tasks as simple as washing dishes, running, listening to music, playing tennis, or fishing, to mention a few. Some people even do their best thinking during the minister's homily on Sunday mornings. You should be alert to activities that get your mind active.

The Quick White Paper

Success is inversely proportional to the thickness of the report.

When you ask yourself how many words it takes to explain success, you quickly realize it takes very few.

When you see a very thick report by a scientist or engineer, what are your feelings? Do you say to yourself, "This person must have failed, now I have to wade through a lengthy explanation of what went wrong."

The engineer or scientist doing the work may believe that failure demands a great deal of explanation because his reputation is at stake. He cannot afford to have people believe that this failure came about through negligence, so he must clearly document the reasons for not succeeding. . . . Somehow we forget that other people can see through this attempt to hide negative results.

On the other hand, producing a very thick report can be an opportunity to impress everyone with the amount of work you did to accomplish your assignment. Too often, the result is that your report becomes one-third fact, one-third fantasy, and one-third balderdash. Once you are caught in this scheme and it usually won't take long, this technique will guarantee that your reports will *not* get read in the future.

Reaction from senior management is rarely positive, even if they never read this report. Senior management may feel, "This person is trying to make sure they have left no stones unturned and he or she turned a few more than were necessary." I once listened to the Chairman of the Board of Directors of one of the world's largest multinational corporation say, "For once I would love to see people present a report without all of the overwhelming detail."

A long report can connote a project as being a failure when it was not. Your readership also might miss the significance of your message, making your effort a failure because you did not get the intended response. Therefore, consider carefully before padding your reports with useless information, hoping merely to impress someone with how much work you did. It will be hard to resist not showing all of your excellent work.

I do not want to dismiss thick reports as being totally out of place. Sometimes they signify a rigorous treatment of a subject, and that can be very positive. Perhaps the usefulness of the data is not fully understood during its collection or there is an invention needed to make the data meaningful. Additional details are sometimes necessary to enhance a report's historical importance.

You can sum up our comments on writing short reports with another writer's adage. *"I wrote you a long letter because I didn't have enough time to write you a short one."*

There should be only one overriding emotion per report.

If you are sitting and listening to a speaker who offers you three central themes to follow, what do you get from the presentation? I am reminded of going to listen to a presentation by a certain professor. This person's entire presentation consisted of quotes from famous people. I found myself wondering just what this speaker personally had to offer for I had no idea of what this particular talk was supposed to convey. I couldn't accept this display of confusion, so I asked, "What do you think on this subject?" I am still waiting for an answer.

This professor had a very high fog factor in snowing people, or was afraid to take any definitive positions. I will grant that this is probably a worst case scenario and most people are not nearly this bad, but it does illustrate how one can spread more confusion than enlightenment by not having one overriding emotion.

You should work hard to leave a clear message in the minds of your audience. If you have more than one message, the audience will have difficulty sorting through your data.

The Quick White Paper

Furthermore, your central theme gets lost in these secondary agendas.

An overriding emotion also culls your data. It forces you to ask, "Does this information support the message I am attempting to convey to my audience?" If data does not support your theme, you should not use it.

When writing a report to senior management and debating putting in a piece of questionable data. . . . Don't! . . . There is another adage that offers guidance here, especially if you are making a presentation to senior management: *"When in doubt, leave it out!"* Reports to senior management should not contain information that you cannot explain. If the data happens to be wrong, your credibility will be lost, and it takes a very long time to regain it.

Furthermore, people feel warmly toward you if they think each paragraph in your article or report is rich with information.

Know the medium through which you intend to publish a given article and the audience background. It will save you from embarrassment and have people raving at your ability to communicate.

Many technical journals make it very clear that they do not want sales articles. These journals are in the business of sharing scientific findings, and they abhor sales types trying to exploit their journals as quasi-sales mediums. The *Journal of the Society of Automotive Engineers* (SAE) is a classic example of a sterile journal used by global corporations to report findings on their internal efforts. The SAE goes so far as to require that an author use only generic names for products to avoid sales pitches for specific brand names.

On the other hand, writing a solely technical article for a media aimed at marketing executives may only find your work dropped into the editor's trash can, and a polite refusal letter.

Quick Writing Adages

Keep in mind that it does not take a major effort to find out something about the readers of your target publication. You can browse through a couple of their past issues to see what they publish.

Lonely? Do you want high-level friends? Then write confidential white papers on non-secure personal computers or workstations, you'll be sure to be noticed.

Today, industrial espionage is a way of life. Trade secrets, such as recipes for new products or strategic directions planned by a corporation, can be worth hundreds of millions of dollars. Its human cost can mean the loss of thousands of jobs as global competitors nibble at your corporation's market share.

Undoubtedly, computers are godsends to the rapid development of your publication, but they are also prime sources for others to steal your confidential ideas and findings. Many people instinctively save their work on a hard-disk drive, for it is very quick and easy to do. Some people also remember to put a password on this information; then they feel reasonably sure that no one can get to their secret. A false sense of security may lead them to tell others that they are working on very confidential projects.

You should keep in mind that good computer hackers garner great pleasure in cracking your password. The best security against this is to say nothing to anyone other than your immediate team members about even the existence of your project. There is an old adage apropos of today's competitive global corporate society: "Loose lips sink ships."

Thus, you should have in place provisions to discard hard copies of your report and to destroy floppy disks used during your writing. *Saving information on the hard disk drive should be kept to a minimum for deleting does not remove it from this disk, especially with modern operating systems that emphasize easy recovery as a feature.* The stationary hard disk

The Quick White Paper

offers a beachhead for a computer hacker to initiate his or her search to locate your information.

We all marvel at how powerful laptop computers have become. Today, high-end laptops rival workstations in their capabilities, and that implies that they are of great interest to industrial spies. If you are writing on a laptop and store your work on its hard disk drive, you offer industrial spies an opportunity to steal your secrets by simply stealing your computer or finding ways to gain access to it while you are, perhaps, out of your hotel room entertaining customers. A good hacker could simply duplicate the information on your hard drive and work on cracking it later.

As laptops move toward having ten giga-byte hard drives in the near future, you want to ask yourself, "Could my corporation afford to lose ten giga-bytes of confidential data?" If you are using your laptop to write confidential reports at home, you may wish to restrict the saving of your reports to floppy disks, CD-Rs, removable hard drives, or transferring to external storage units that remain at your home.

Imagine the reaction reflected in your workmates' faces if they found out that your carelessness caused corporate secrets to be stolen by foreign competitors and that, in turn, could cost them their jobs. There is no doubt that you would have a difficult go of it with people knowing you caused the latest round of corporate downsizing at your corporation.

User-friendly articles and reports get read more often than stereotypical technocratic-drab.

User-friendliness is the most difficult aspect of technical writing, for it requires you to have an understanding of the subject matter and a willingness to share this information with a mass audience. Both of these conditions are necessary for you to write something that is user-friendly.

Quick Writing Adages

If you have a case where someone truly understands his or her subject matter yet feels insecure in their position, that person usually becomes expert at gobbledegook. I once visited a customer accompanied by a chap that everyone said was a genius, yet after my associate left, I spent the next three months translating his presentation to the customer. The words of the customer still ring in my mind: "What did he say?"

Yet this same chap refused to offer any assistance that allowed one to truly understand his research work. His reluctance to share data and understanding brought into question his true worth to the organization and made me wonder if he maintained a high fog factor to purposefully keep the company from making a cost/benefit analysis on his projects.

On the other hand, you hear people comment, "I was totally lost while listening to that presentation, and there was no doubt in my mind that the speaker had no idea what he or she was doing." It is embarrassing to see a person writing about something he or she knows nothing about and having someone else point out the writer's ignorance? People in the scientific community are not bashful when they think you are wrong. I learned this at an international conference on Solid State Physics when a world renowned physicist corrected a chap's paper on the stage. That person left the stage totally disgraced.

A similar situation occurs during internal presentations and reports when some scientist or engineer publishes questionable data that some senior member in his/her organization knows is wrong. Or they may have incomplete data that does not answer the question that management posed for their research. In each case, the researcher is *de facto* lying, for he/she is knowingly presenting false information to his/her management.

The Quick White Paper

Thus, if you decide that a key goal of your work is for your extended audience to be able to use your data immediately, user-friendliness becomes a labor of love. If you are making a theoretical derivation, add the couple of extra lines that will save the reader valuable time trying to work through your calculations.

User-friendliness implies that you stay focussed on the issue at hand. This will avoid confusing the reader while you engage in a digression that may add very little value to your article or report. Remember people instinctively gauge the success of your work by its brevity, so you do not want them to ignore your paper or report because you're padding it with confusing and irrelevant information.

User-friendly can also apply to the language used to write your report or article. While working for the Du Pont Company, I experimented with using my journalistic experience to make technical reports readable as well as to produce them very quickly. When my reviewer read my earlier reports, he had complained about my writing style. My goal was to make a paradigm shift in the readability of technical reports, so I set about utilizing the system herein described. Over time our technical director commented to me how much he enjoyed reading my technical reports.

My focus was to take complicated ideas and break them down as I would if I were writing a newspaper column. The key goal was to have the audience understand my research and to report only the significant data needed to make my case.

It became apparent that *writing in the active voice turned dull reading into interesting material.* This style of writing makes the reader feel the action is occurring today and not something that was done a hundred years ago.

I also found that paragraphs should average three to four sentences in length with a maximum of six sentences.

The font should be 12 points for ease of reading. Each sentence should average no more than five lines on 8 1/2 by 11 inch (22 x 28 cm) paper with a one inch (2.5 cm) margin at the top, bottom, left, and right.

A picture is still worth a thousand words.

Graphics negate the need to use several pages of text to visualize difficult concepts. They also transcend language barriers within your corporation or at international conferences.

Graphics can be tables, charts, and/or pictures within the same document. More than one central idea per chart can lead your audience to erroneous conclusions. Whenever possible, put a conclusion below the graphic. This will insure that the reader will come to your desired conclusion and not merely interpret your findings for himself.

Significant care should be taken in making charts, graphs, and tables. You want to avoid making "pretty" charts that say nothing substantive. Hype is acceptable in advertising, but it is not relished by hard nosed managers expecting something concrete for making business decisions.

On the other hand, charts that are too difficult to understand or are overloaded with information will seriously limit the audience's receptivity to your paper or report. Senior level managers may also chastise you for wasting their time plowing through your work. People listening as you present "busy" charts may spend all of their time trying to discern what the charts are showing and ignore what you are saying.

Remember, your goal is to produce a document that is readable by your target audience. That suggests that it is better to err on the side of having too many simple charts than to have too few very complicated ones.

This is also an excellent opportunity to instill an image of your research goals into the minds of your audience. It gives you the chance to say, "My work is ready for immediate use in enhancing the business."

The Quick White Paper

Doing business in the global marketplace now demands that you know and use international units.

Imagine. . . . giving a scientific presentation to a group of engineers in a foreign country. You are quite proud of your findings, and you are sure that these strangers will embrace your ideas for these ideas should significantly improve their competitiveness.

You open by saying, "We increased the burst pressure on our hose from 5000 psi to 8000 psi." You know they don't speak English so you wait for the interpreter to translate your message. When he or she is finished, you notice that there are blank stares looking up at you. "What did I do wrong?" you think to yourself.

You continue, "We also reduced the weight per foot by 0.15 pounds." The interpreter tries again to convey your message. Again you see blank stares.

The interpreter does not want to embarrass you, so he or she allows you to continue. Somehow you get through your presentation based on the polite smiles from your audience. They don't ask any questions, for their culture demands that the audience make an effort to understand the information that the speaker is giving, in his or her presentation.

As you prepare to leave, you wonder why no one asked for a sample of your product. You wait for someone to say something, but nothing happens. Your interpreter then thanks your host for allowing you to speak, and you all politely leave.

You review your visit trying to discern what went wrong. The blank stares in the customers' faces are now haunting your mind. Then you realize that the puzzled expressions meant that these foreign customers had no idea what you were speaking about. They understand units such as bar, mega Pascal, meter, and kilogram — not pounds per square inch, inch, foot or pound.

Quick Writing Adages

You just received a tough lesson in communicating in the world marketplace, for you wasted a great deal of your corporation's resources to sponsor your foreign trip and produced no return on their investment. A little forethought could have made this a successful trip. You should have created charts and graphs using units that could be understood by your intended audience. This is also true for internal corporate reports where one must present findings in a manner that is usable by the corporation's global family membership.

Therefore, if you use the appropriate units, your article or report is ready for the world marketplace. You will also find today that many publications are demanding that international units be used in all articles.

Develop your report to the highest standard of excellence needed for your potential audience and you only need to write your work once to meet the requirements of all media.

Some people will tell you that a given report does not require a very high standard of accuracy, so you might offer your audience rough data or promise to correct it later. These statements are fine if you expect your work to have only limited exposure to non-decision-making individuals and a brief shelf life (period before being trashed).

If there is even a remote possibility that your work will land in front of a senior manager or might become a part of a retrievable database system, you need to make certain that this work represents your highest calibre of performance. This technique will also give you the added ability to generate ancillary documents, presentations, and trade articles very quickly since the data is readily portable.

In my last year at the DuPont Company, I was in the midst of preparing a technical paper to present to the Society of Automotive Engineers in early March when I learned that another chap could not honor a request to the Detroit Rubber

The Quick White Paper

Group a subdivision of the Rubber Division of the American Chemical Society. I found myself burdened with two technical papers on two different subjects within a two-week period.

The first paper was well underway, but the research on the second paper needed finalizing. The initial effort on the first paper took the form of writing the trade paper for the Society of Automotive Engineers within the guidelines of the company's internal technical report format. I, therefore, had a document that had portability and could be readily modified to meet restrictions placed on my findings by management and the legal department.

Since time was my worst enemy, I worked on the second article in a joint arrangement with another scientist who had conducted the research we intended to use to demonstrate the superiority of our product over a multinational competitor's product. We were a good team for I understood the trade needs from my own research efforts; my coauthor understood our product's superior traits and had data to demonstrate them.

I exploited the internal technical reporting system to lay out this second research paper in a short time period using the known information. My coauthor completed his internal measurements, and we produced the internal technical report, including all approvals for presentation to the Detroit Rubber Group, in roughly five weeks.

Using the existing company technical reporting system as a template for an external research paper reduced the stress of developing a new paper quickly, as our effort became one of filling in the blanks. This system also allowed us to get a peer review of our efforts while we were still writing the paper. Therefore, we only needed to present a final draft to our management for approval. We made all of our management-suggested corrections in one day, for we had the paper in our own computer. We had little problem meeting our presentation schedule.

Quick Writing Adages

I had planned to give a last paper to close out my technical marketing career with the DuPont Company in November of 1993, the month of my retirement. I was to give the same paper at the Fall meeting of the International Society of Industrial Fabric Manufacturers as well as Textile World's "Textiles in Automotives" Fall '93 Conference. However, there was a need to give an additional paper at the Textile World conference.

I exploited the portability of works done with high calibre software on personal computers. By simply making minor modifications in the charts on behalf of my new audience, the second paper and its presentation charts were completed in a couple of hours. Thus, I gave two consecutive papers on two different subjects on the same day.

The key issues here are aiming your writing at the highest level of potential audiences and developing ancillaries on systems that offer you the maximum in portability.

Using Windows or Macintosh-based computing systems eases the wear on your nerves.

One of the key elements in writing technical papers, internal and trade presentations, and technical reports quickly is the portability of data between applications.

Suppose your boss asked you to make a presentation on findings you reported in your technical report to both management and operators at a couple of your plant sites. In generating your initial paper, you worked in the *Windows* framework where you made your tables in *Excel*, developed the graphics in *Freelance*, and composed your documents in *WordPerfect*.

You can now exchange items between these high-end programs; therefore, if you saved your original work on disk, you can simply call it up and insert the charts you need. Hence, having written your initial work at the highest possible

The Quick White Paper

level now offers you the flexibility to exploit cut-and-paste techniques to develop a host of targeted reports and presentations.

To become proficient in generating quick reports, you should consider obtaining a working knowledge of word processing, database, graphics, and spreadsheet programs running under the *Windows* or the *Macintosh* format. This knowledge allows you to do in hours, with a high degree of accuracy, jobs that would take days to do without such programs.

Working with your data gives an excellent insight into reality.

Most people desire to have some status in life. As we work at our professions, we expect to become recognized for our contributions, and we want the perks that tell the public we have arrived. We use earned degrees, patents, publications, and so on to gauge our value to the organization.

But this ego building has a downside that is very costly to the company. If we allow ego blindness to encourage us to merely get our assistants to rack up data and offer us only summaries, our corporation loses the quality of our expertise and our quickness at solving problems.

When you are working through your raw data, you develop a sense for what it says. You also recognize when it is insufficient to answer the questions posed to you by management; if so, you can establish a new series of tests where needed.

Little subtleties that can go unnoticed in summaries can be very significant in interpreting the data. The recognition of these subtleties can mean the difference between average and excellent research reports. Nevertheless, it is easy to have technicians collect data and rack it up into nice, neat charts. This takes less time on your part. If you have merely one or

Quick Writing Adages

two pieces of data, this system is fine, but you may sacrifice those subtleties.

Whenever there is a considerable amount of data for analysis, you may find having your assistant do all of the tabulation helps these employees have a good appreciation of the test results, but it does little for you, the principal researcher. You gave away a golden opportunity to get an in-depth understanding of what the numbers and pictures convey.

In any case, you will find it rewarding to take the time to see that your technicians or assistants are trained to understand your research effort. They should understand your test results, for that offers you an extra trained mind to comment on your findings. Technicians often see things that will elude your eyes, especially if the project is very large with many sets of data.

Some food for thought for gaining good participation from technicians or assistants follows:

A) Let the technicians know that they are not merely sets of hands to perform menial tasks, but they are true members of your research team, replete with ideas to make the venture go. Most people like to feel they are needed, so you should expect significant cooperation once the technicians are certain that you are serious about their participation.

B) Teach technicians how to write, give internal and trade presentations, and understand research reports. It is good if you require them to make a couple of presentations, for only then will they fully comprehend the importance of having accurate and timely data.

C) Require technicians to write down any observations or comments they have on the data outside of the stan-

The Quick White Paper

dard replies requested on test forms. This permits the technician to have a good understanding of his or her results and encourages attention to detail.

I received excellent dividends from their cooperation by having highly trained technicians while I was working in private industry. Some key dividends which you can expect to gain are:

1) Insurance of a very high degree of accuracy in the measurements when you cannot be present to observe the experiment. Technicians quickly learn that it is not possible to defend poor quality measurements, so they will not take short cuts as opposed to accepted practices for obtaining accurate data.

2) Technicians develop a full appreciation of the projects. They feel like a member of the team rather than like a robot merely programmed by the researcher.

3) Well trained technicians can easily pull together data for reports and presentations via telephone.

4) New insights on the data often emerge that you did not note or consider.

5) Technicians give a 110 percent effort in making a project a success when they have a personal interest in it.

If you personally observe an experiment, you know the difference between fact and fantasy.

It is common practice for many engineers and scientists to write-up a work request for experiments then sit and await the results. Technicians often make notes on the report to

Quick Writing Adages

describe what happens. If you are running a routine test, these technician notes may be more than adequate to meet your needs. However, if you are on the forefront of knowledge, there is no substitute for seeing the experiment run personally.

This first hand observation offers an opportunity to modify the test if something is wrong. It also gives an understanding of the details of the test effort and potential problems.

Your personal experience in observing test runs offers you a quantum leap in understanding when it comes time to analyze the data. You have a clear picture of the problem areas in your mind. It is also a key ingredient in the recipe for quick writing; for doubt in your mind can encumber your ability to write. There is an adage that says, *"Doubt is a veil over your mind, but confidence is the light that guides you through ignorance."*

Analyzing your data today prevents tomorrow's confusion and anxiety from mental overload.

The importance of understanding your data cannot be overemphasized in quick writing. Therefore, one must look for every opportunity to foster that understanding, often doing small things that reduce the complexity of the issues that are before us.

If you immediately write a few data analysis statements at the bottom of each sheet of data, you will find this data has instant value as a writing tool. It is also meaningful to other people who may view this effort. By adding these immediate assessments to your work, you have prevented reams of new data from turning into a mass of confusion.

Should you opt not to make an immediate assessment of the data, you may find yourself struggling to recall just what

The Quick White Paper

you were doing. Therefore, you have introduced doubt, and that turns your writing effort into a real chore. Making interim notes during the investigation provides a basis from which to take a holistic look at the information, regardless of whether the premises of your research remain the same.

A thoughtful data summary is a hologram of your effort.

Writing is nothing more than words that create a picture of an emotion in your mind. Text, tables, and charts are merely a foundation for your ideas. They give them life and make others more accepting of your feelings. Thus, an excellent summary of your research effort seeks to make your audience share in your conviction.

An excellent summary is a necessary item if you are to have a ghost of a chance at rapid writing. This summary will allow you to write internal reports and presentations at the same time. With a good word processing program such as *WordPro*, *WordPerfect* or *Word*, statements from a research report can be copied to a presentation framework and minor modifications made to the information as necessary. This technique allows you to generate presentations for management or customers very quickly.

If you admit, "I don't know," no one will make a fool of you.

One of the most difficult things for many people to do is to admit that they don't know everything. Somehow we believe we must be omnipotent, or we appear weak. This thinking is absolute suicide when it comes to quick writing, for you are no longer writing with a clear understanding of purpose. You are now moving from the realm of technical writing to fiction writing, for what you say may simply not be true.

Persons with in-depth knowledge of your field will recognize your futile attempt at fiction in a nonfiction arena, and they may take you to task for your liberal interpretation of the facts. Senior managers will not be kind should they find out that you misrepresented the facts.

If you point out that you don't know something but will research it further at a later date, you will find it forms closure on questions and retains your credibility. If you say "I don't know," you have not committed a crime. If you say that we are continuing our research in this area to attempt to answer some obvious questions, that leaves the reader yearning for your next work.

However, if you are a know-it-all, you may find your audience giving you enough rope to hang yourself and then taking great pleasure in your demise. Why lose your valuable credibility with ego blindness that will disappear in a few moments?

Copying at least two sets of your report during its writing on floppy disk, and storing them in different locations, eliminates writer's paranoia over the potential of your computer crashing or a natural disaster destroying your work.

Whenever we write very large reports, we find ourselves protecting this work in hard copies and disk copies. We know that the potential for a disaster is always present, and we hate to think that our great effort fell victim to one. Subtle pressures such as this weigh heavily on your mind when you are trying to write, they cloud your thinking, a taboo to quick writing.

We are merely contending that you follow the old adage, "An ounce of prevention is worth a pound of cure."

Chapter IV

TECHNICAL REPORT ELEMENTS DEFINED

We are now ready to start the actual writing effort. We will take the issues we discussed thus far and quickly create reports that our management will find very useful in running the corporation.

We heretofore established the elements of a technical report writing template that possesses the power to generate papers quickly. But we never defined these elements in a manner useful to scientists and engineers.

Since a single picture is often worth a thousand words, recall the *Technical Report Elements* writing model below. It contains the key report elements for developing a comprehensive technical report that fits most corporate technical research writing needs.

The Quick White Paper

We will examine each element by defining it and, where appropriate, will offer actual examples from published papers. Although these elements may contain confidential material, we shall only touch on this issue with brief statements, for confidentiality is unique to a given corporation.

Our efforts will focus on your learning to use the report writing template as the master guide to generate a high calibre research report that has portable elements. With such, you can freely extract whatever elements necessary to generate other reports or presentations that address specific requests from your management.

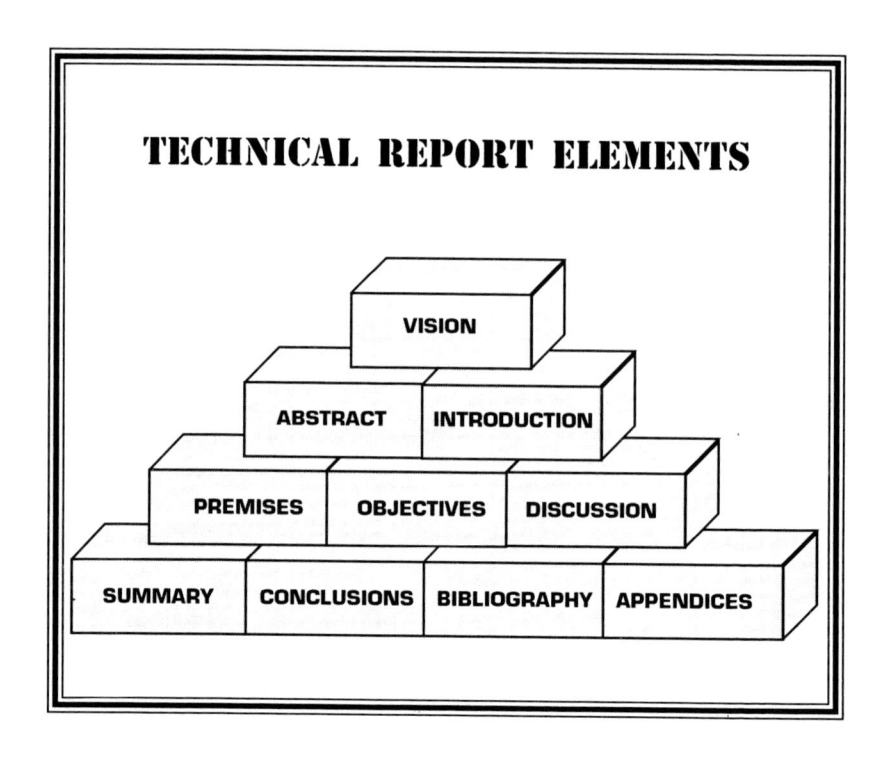

TECHNICAL REPORT ELEMENTS

```
                    VISION
            ABSTRACT    INTRODUCTION
      PREMISES   OBJECTIVES   DISCUSSION
  SUMMARY   CONCLUSIONS   BIBLIOGRAPHY   APPENDICES
```

VISION STATEMENT

What do we mean by vision?

Vision, simply put, is the mental picture of how you want things to be when your report is read by your audience. Perhaps you visualize your report being embraced by your management or peers, so that your research credibility is enhanced by your unique findings. You may be saving thousands of jobs because your invention offers the corporation a whole new market segment to enter. Or it can be that your invention causes a paradigm shift in thinking in a given field.

In a less grandiose manner, you may want to show that money is being wasted on the current production process; and you have a new method that will save millions of dollars for your corporation. Perhaps you are providing management with a response to a strategic or tactical objective in the business plan.

Vision is that dream in your mind of what you hope to see tomorrow. In the technical paper that we touched on earlier, "Systematic Techniques of Hose Failure Mode Analysis," the vision was simply to develop a systematic technique for doing free length (2.54 cm from the hose coupling) hose failure analyses. The hose literature contained papers that talked about hose failure analysis but none offered a recipe for conducting one.

You should be able to write down your vision statement in one sentence or within three at most. This vision statement is the key element in your report writing. Once you have a clear idea of what you want to accomplish, you can decide quickly the things you require to achieve your dream. Therefore, you want to take as much time as necessary to develop an excellent vision statement with which you feel comfortable.

The Quick White Paper

Attempting to write without first establishing a clear vision statement is tantamount to walking into several shopping malls merely to look at the merchandise, in the hope that some divine revelation will suggest what you should buy. On the other hand, if you need a new pair of shoes, you know to focus your visit on shoe stores. You may ignore other stores, but there is no doubt that wasted time at the mall is kept to a minimum.

It is safe to say *the time spent developing your vision statement will be paid back tenfold in reduced frustration when it comes time to write your report.*

Imagine. . . . you are confronted with having to report on an experiment that failed. You are haunted by the adage, "*Success has many friends but failure has none.*" Do you report bad findings in today's world and risk being labeled a failure? You feel great stress, for you know that failures enhance your chances of becoming a victim of corporate downsizing in the next round of rationalization.

The temptation is great to find a way to merely change the rules in your favor. An example of using deception to cover up the failure in your research effort is seen in your playing the game of unofficially restating your objectives.

Perhaps your management gave you an objective that read: "Develop a new aqueous adhesion system that improves the adhesion level of natural rubber to nylon by 20 percent by the end of September 1998." October 1998 rolls around and you are asked to give a program review on your work to management in early November. This request is disquieting for you know that your efforts were a failure.

You are upset over the potential of losing your job because you have only bad results to report. You must now fight off the urge to deceive by merely rewriting the objective to make your findings palatable. A simple restatement such as, "Explore new dip systems for nylon that offer potentially improved adhesion levels of 20 percent" would be fine.

In this new framework, you can ballyhoo your findings of a 5 percent increase in adhesion, and subtly suggest that the 20 percent figure was too high. You feel good, for you know that they usually kill the messenger bearing bad news, and your message is now a positive one.

However, your deception may lead to another research effort in the future that rekindles the old objective, if it is of great importance to your corporation. Your present research efforts may get overlooked by the new researcher, for you attempted to distance yourself from the original goal your management had in mind. This may lessen the value of your research to future scientists and engineers.

Surely you will agree that the above research reporting deception leads to a serious waste of corporate resources and jeopardizes the corporation's existence in the future. It also implies that *management wants to insure there exists an atmosphere that fosters intellectual honesty, so that today's research efforts guarantee tomorrow's corporate prosperity.*

ABSTRACT

Technical papers usually start with an a*bstract that is a single paragraph meant to encourage the reader to read the paper by providing a capsule summary of the work.* When librarians do a literature search on a particular subject, they supply the abstract to researchers, who rely upon it to decide if the article or report is pertinent to their effort. This suggests that your abstract must be very informative on the findings reported in your article or technical report.

Abstracts are often upper management's vehicle to assess your research, for they do not wish to read long dissertations

The Quick White Paper

to glean an understanding of the business significance of your effort. Since the abstract is an efficient way of communicating with senior management, you want to take extra care that the information provided in it also addresses their needs.

There are three key elements in an abstract that make it a good vehicle for technical searches and an effective tool to meet the business needs of senior management. It should *offer a rationale for why you did the work, list the tests performed, and provide the scientific and/or business results* from your effort.

a) RATIONALE

Businesses have a responsibility to shareholders to make a profit and not function merely as social organizations to solve the world's problems. Therefore, expenditures of corporate resources need to be justified when you present your report. This justification shows that your efforts were a wise use of company resources.

The first statement in the abstract should center on a rationale for your research that has management viewing your report in a positive light. You might use a rationale statement similar to this one that reads, "Constant complaints in the hose industry about blown-off fittings on high pressure hoses reinforced with nylon required a closer examination of the lateral properties of the reinforcement cord filaments to understand their contribution to premature hose fitting failures."

The above statement points out that there are complaints in the high pressure hose industry over fitting failures. Perhaps a hose design engineer is trying to make hoses out of aramid, polyester or some new polymer where he or she is finding fitting failures, and your work can provide guidance in his research efforts. Your work shared the importance of the filament lateral modulus in maintaining hose fitting retention, an idea that had never crossed the mind of most hose design engineers.

b) TEST PROGRAM

If you ran tests, you should state the nature of them. You might write something like, "Used photomicrographic studies of nylon filaments to study bundle shapes after exposure to a lateral axis crushing force of 10 newton per square millimeter."

You are telling the reader that you examined the filaments under a microscope to look for damage, and you took pictures of what you saw. This tells the reader to expect some pictures that show your findings.

However, in cases where your work is a theoretical treatise, you will want to highlight your ability to calculate different variables as opposed to the need to use valuable resources to produce test items.

c) RESULTS

The results are the ultimate justification of your work, for they tell management that you responded to a need. You either accomplished their mission or their goal was beyond the scope of present technology. Thus, management will look for definitive conclusions and should not get a sense that you are waffling, for that would suggest that your findings are suspect.

You might write a results statement as follows: "Found radial cracks and a permanent bundle deformation that reduced the normal force component in the frictional force used to retain the hose fitting."

You have now told the reader that in textile hose reinforcements the fitting is held on by frictional force, and

The Quick White Paper

the normal force component necessary for producing this force is changing. This should pique the reader's interest to want to know if such things as time and temperature are important here.

An example of a complete abstract is as follows:

"Hose manufacturers constantly seek better techniques for assessing their hose economics. They are also using more and more textile reinforcements to produce hoses to meet demanding applications in automotive and industrial markets. Thus, hose manufacturers need a set of equations that permits them to do paper studies on textile hose designs to avoid the costly process of making each item. Equations, derived from empirical data on PPD-T aramid, nylon, polyester, and MPD-T aramid, for knitted hose economics are offered. There are also equations offered to estimate the cord gauge that is a necessary input for calculating innerliner coverage in knit, spiral, and braided hoses. Having a good estimate of the cord gauge is very important in obtaining good hose burst pressure because low inner-liner pack leads to pinhole failures. On the other hand, overpack can cause delamination without secondary adhesion systems present."

A second abstract example is:

"Systematic techniques to analyze industrial and automotive hose failures are presented. End use requirements for textile reinforcement cords versus hose specifications and end use operating environments are assessed. Hose design criteria are examined from a reverse engineering manner. The Facts Mapping technique is offered as a vehicle to manage the data generated in the failure analysis. A definition of a hose failure is offered. Proper selections of the hose inner-liner and cover materials and the reinforcement cord are emphasized."

A third abstract example is:

> "Filament transverse properties of hose reinforcement cords are given to assess their potential impact on hose fitting retention during its end use life. Comparative properties of commercial para-aramid homopolymer and para-aramid copolymer offer some insight on the risk of fitting failures between these high strength aramid products. Actual field testing of a high pressure hose suggests superior fitting retention with the para-aramid homopolymer."

It is important to note that we included both technical and business data in abstracts. Your senior management can use your abstract to get a thumbnail sketch of your work without being bogged down in a great deal of detail.

In reports written solely for internal consumption, you may want to include the business significance of your research effort in the abstract. Statements such as "Increased sales potential by five million dollars. . . ." grab management's attention and aid in their making a quick mental cost/benefit analysis of your effort. These are statements that you will want to remove should you rewrite your original report for outside consumption and transfer the non-confidential material from this internal report to a trade article or trade presentation.

REPORT INTRODUCTION

In the introduction you survey the literature, pointing out what has been done in the past and how your work contributes to new learning. This avoids your coming out with a "me-too article" that will only put your audience to sleep because it offers nothing novel.

In an internal confidential report, you will want to use the introduction section to justify your research effort to your management. They expect you to offer the business significance of your effort here. You need to speak to meeting strategic or tactical objectives such as increased sales, or defending your existing product line against attacks by competitors.

The introduction also helps you avoid wasting time and money when answers to the questions posed by your management already exist. Often, completing a search of the current literature requires that you work closely with your librarian, for references are not always easy to locate. Sometimes you find that there are articles that need translating unless you have expertise in the language of the publication.

A historical approach, giving excerpts from a series of articles that lead up to your present work, is a straightforward way of writing an introduction. You are simply placing things in chronological order, thereby highlighting a chasm in the literature that you intend to fill. The introduction should be of sufficient length to bring out the key articles that offer credibility to your research effort.

An example of an effective introduction is:

> "Traditional thinking says when end-users consider high pressure hose applications, they envision purchasing either braided or spiral reinforced steel wire hoses. The higher operating pressure these hoses must have, the greater the number of spiral or braid plaits reinforcing them. Numerous reinforcement layers can make steel reinforced hoses difficult to handle because of high weight per unit hose length and unnecessary high hose stiffness.
>
> "Today hose manufacturers can produce high pressure aramid reinforced hoses at a fraction of the weight of steel reinforced hoses. DuPont offers Kevlar® that is several times stronger than steel on an equal weight basis. However, the use of aramids in producing high pressure hoses requires different design considerations versus steel wire reinforcement.

Report Elements Defined

"A key area of difference is in the joining of the hose and the fitting in the coupling operation. A survey of the literature offers some insight on the present thinking surrounding the interaction of the fitting and the hose components.

"The decay of stress within a coupling is fairly fast to a much lower level than that achieved during the swaging and the final value is greatly dependent upon the properties of the elastomer being compressed and the design of fitting," writes Colin W. Evans.

"Evans highlights the importance of stress decay and suggests that it is a function of the elastomer and the fitting design, thus implying that the reinforcement does not contribute to the stress decay. This thinking fits the wire model but it may not fit the textile reinforcement model.

"V.V. Arkhipov argues, '... The contact stresses that ensure the strength and hermetic sealing of the hose connection depend on the extent of deformation of the hose wall by the components of the connecting fitting. As for the degree of hose wall compression to ensure work capacity of the hose with the fitting, there is no agreed opinion: it is recommended only for compressive fittings, and according to various data, fluctuates from 20 to 70%. ...'

"Arkhipov's statement highlights the significance of frictional forces in the hose fitting retention. It also suggests that affixing the fitting to the hose is an art in which one needs to run test series to establish optimum swage constriction levels.

"Patrick J. Lee reports, '... Manufacturers now are developing non-skive coupling for spiral wire hoses. In these designs the ferrule on the coupling penetrates the hose cover to grip the wire reinforcement, leaving the tube intact for sealing.'

"This statement suggests that compressional decay in the cover jacket has shifted its role in fitting retention because the ferrule is in direct contact with the wire reinforcement; therefore, the cover jacket now is relegated to being a sealant in the fitting.

"'Anchorage of the ferrule to the hose was achieved by the internal threads of the ferrule gripping onto the wire reinforcement which had been bared. ... Anchorage to the hose is achieved by means of formed teeth on the ferrule

The Quick White Paper

which penetrated the hose cover and bite onto the wire reinforcement,' wrote David Catterall.

"Catterall's comments make clear that the hose manufacturers expect high pressure hose reinforcements to also act as quasi-screw shafts on which to affix the fitting. That is, the ferrule will penetrate into the wire reinforcement bundle and not merely apply a crushing force to it.

"The literature suggests the existence of a pervasive wire reinforcement mind set in the development of techniques for producing high pressure hoses. But the growth of high strength textiles in these high pressure hose applications demands a reassessment of some staid hose fitting design principles. There is now a need to understand key textile reinforcement physical properties that contribute to the hose fitting retention.

"Thus, this work will assess the importance of transverse filament properties of high strength textile reinforcement cords used in or being considered as potential candidates for high pressure hose applications."

Clearly, you can see this introduction allowed us to mix marketing and technical objectives in the same article. If you submitted this same introduction statement to the Society of Automotive Engineers, they would most likely request that you revise it to eliminate the specific product name of Kevlar® and use it's generic name, para-aramid. This suggests that you also might consider more liberal publications for including both technical and marketing objectives in your external works.

Another example of a trade paper introduction statement is:

"Today's automobile designers place more stringent requirements on hoses used in the engine compartment. The hose manufacturer must now produce products that can withstand engine compartment temperatures of 150 degrees Centigrade.

"High temperature environments require the hose manufacturer to consider meta and para aramids to reinforce critical automotive hoses. Nomex® aramid is a prime

Report Elements Defined

reinforcement for automobile heater hoses in cars produced in the United States. Kevlar® aramid reinforces radiator hoses made for both the European and the U. S. markets.

"Selling prices per pound (kilogram) of meta and para aramids are significantly higher than for nylon, polyester, and rayon. Therefore, hose manufacturers seek theoretical ways to assess cord content before undertaking new projects. Equations presented in this paper help the hose design engineer to make cost comparison studies on new and existing reinforcement materials.

"Colin Evans[1] offers a hose burst equation for knitted hoses. Yet the hose manufacturer needs to predict the weight of the reinforcement per unit hose length to calculate the cost of a new hose design.

"Hose engineers also want to estimate the effect of the reinforcement gauge on inner-liner coverage. This relationship helps to determine openness of the coverage for strike-through adhesion. Poor strike-through adhesion leads to delamination of the cover jacket in hose use.

"David J. Spencer[2] offers equations for knitted fabric tightness or compactness. He also gives an equation for the total area covered by a cord. But his equations require one to have a constant (K) for the reinforcement involved.

"Miller[3] offers the hose design engineer a set of equations for making paper studies on knitted automotive hoses. It uses numerical values easily obtained from hose measurements.

"Yet, traditionally, yarns used in Mechanical Rubber Goods (MRG) applications evolved from Tire Cord applications. If the yarn proved itself acceptable for tires, it was generally felt to be satisfactory for MRG. This meant that tests for MRG cords often followed a tire cord format.

"In tire cords, one wants excellent fatigue life from cords because a tire undergoes millions of revolutions during a life time. To get the level of fatigue necessary requires the inclusion of twist in the cord. To insure good fatigue life a 6.5 twist multiplier cord (T.M. = Turns Per Meter Times Square Root (Dtex) divided by 3000, or Turns per Inch Times square root (Denier) divided by 73[4]) is used. This twist level also offers a cord bundle that has a cylindrical appearance.

The Quick White Paper

"A cylindrical appearance is the basis for calculating the cord gauge. The cord gauge is defined as the diameter of the twisted cord structure. The 6.5 twist multiplier for tires is too high for many hose applications because there is considerable loss in tensile strength with increasing twist level. For synthetic yarns like Kevlar® aramid, Dacron® polyester, and nylon, roughly 1.1 twist multiplier will offer the highest break strength cord. This low level of twist will not produce the cylindrical bundle commonplace with high twist yarn. This poses the question of what is the proper cord gauge for hose applications requiring a low twist cord.

"In hose applications, it is important to know how well the cords cover the inner-liner to assess the potential for pinhole cracks by the liner drawing up into the interstitial openings between cord lays. The percent pack offers an assessment of the size of these interstices. Hose manufacturers may use the trade standard percent pack equation for spiral and braided hose to make pack assessments. However, cord gauge measurements for this equation centered on an assumed cylindrical bundle cross section

"Miller's pack equation for plain stitch knitted hoses also calls for knowing the cord gauge of a low twist cord bundle that is known to have a non-cylindrical bundle shape. DuPont International made knitted Kevlar® hose (see Appendix I) of the same denier yarn with 0.0, 120, and 160 turns per meter twist levels that shows a significant decrease in inner-liner coverage with increasing twist level. This picture corroborates the need to understand the noncylindrical bundle model in hose applications.

"Intuitively, low twist cords would be expected to form a ribbonlike cross section with a major and minor bundle axis. This makes calculations based on the cylindrical cord model fail to consider the importance of bundle shape in gauge assessments where the major bundle width defines the cord gauge. In defining the gauge, the major bundle width determines the inner-liner percent coverage. This present work also uses empirical data to derive simple equations for calculating Kevlar®, Dacron®, and nylon cord bundle width from knowing the cord denier (dtex), substrate fiber density, and the cord bundle packing factor (filament fiber area / bundle face area)."

PREMISES

Premises are the scientific or business assumptions you make when you set out to do your work. They are especially important in theoretical works for setting up your equations. However, you will find on occasion that your premises are wrong once you have the data to test them. You should not be afraid to acknowledge that you had to revise your premises, for you want to maintain your integrity for high calibre research.

You may want to use implied versus overt premises when you are developing your paper. The key issue to keep in mind is, "Does the reader understand my assumptions?" If you worry that the reader does not appreciate your assumptions, you might opt for overt premises.

The premises section of the Detroit Rubber Group paper reads as follows:

> "An assessment of the literature and discussions with hose industry experts suggest a set of premises for coupling textile reinforced high pressure hoses.
>
> They are:
>
> 1. Frictional force is the dominant force in fitting retention.
>
> 2. If the ferrule is screwed into the filament bundle, it could cause a significant loss of reinforcement cord tensile strength increasing the potential of hose fitting failures.
>
> 3. Filament transverse tensile modulus is a key contributor to the compressional force necessary for fitting retention.
>
> 4. Hose fitting design is a proprietary art of the fitting manufacturers.

The Quick White Paper

> 5. Adhesion between both the cover jacket and the inner-liner with the reinforcement for elastomeric compounds is necessary to avoid unnecessary displacement of the liner during swaging."

The focus of the above premises is on an experimental effort. You will note a different slant in ones intended for theoretical calculations. They highlight the importance of premises in deriving equations because you must have a foundation upon which to build your mathematical model.

The following came from the paper entitled, "Knitted Heater Hose Static Equations: Burst Pressure and Economics":

> "... To derive the above equation required adopting three premises. They are:
>
> 1. Cord bundle cross section area remained constant regardless of cord tension and simulated inner-liner outside diameter.
>
> 2. Cord bundle modification (aspect) ratio is greater than 1.
>
> 3. Cord gauge is a function of the bundle modification ratio, denier (dtex), and cord density.
>
> "The first premise addressed what happens to the cord bundle when the reinforcement cord undergoes tensioning while it is around the inner-liner. Previous work assumed the face area of the cord bundle remains constant. Since the cord length remains unchanged, the constant face area assumption utilizes the rationale of Poisson's ratio where the total bundle volume remains constant after the material deforms."
>
> "The second premise merely implies that the bundle will not be round. A round bundle has a modification ratio of 1 and is indicative of high twisted cord.
>
> "The third premise spells out the key cord bundle factors believed related to its gauge."

OBJECTIVES

Objectives are strategic and tactical statements that spell out the desires of your management; your work is usually responding to one of these desires. They usually contain a statement that identifies a need to be accomplished, a time for the project completion, and the person or organization responsible for completing the assignment.

Objectives will best serve you in internal reports to management or presentations to specific customers where you agreed to undertake a project to obtain answers to questions they deemed important. They will most often fall under the category of confidential information that you want to purge when developing external publications for public consumption.

One word of caution: *You want to bear in mind that strategic objectives should be given only to people on a "need to know" basis.* This suggests that you want to make certain that you do not reveal them in open meetings to impress your underlings, thereby making the work of industrial spies easier.

DISCUSSION

The *Discussion* section gives you an opportunity to present your findings in detail. *This is where you discuss your test design, make your calculations, and present your data.* You are providing information that shows how you met the goal that you raised in the *Introduction* section.

There are many ways to layout the discussion section, but the following subareas are present in many reports:

    a) Opening Comments
    b) Background
    c) Test Outline
    d) Data
    e) Results

The Quick White Paper

a) OPENING COMMENTS

Opening comments are your last ditch effort to capture your reader's mind to spend the time necessary to read through the material you are about to present. These statements restate succinctly ideas that you presented elsewhere in the report but are worthy of repetition.

An example of an opening comment is:

> "Du Pont's initial study of automotive coolant and heater hoses focused on knitted heater hoses. In this effort Du Pont examined hose construction parameters in both static and dynamic tests on hoses reinforced with Nomex®, Kevlar®, and Technora® aramid. . . .
> "Although Du Pont ran both static and dynamic tests on knitted heater hoses, this paper will only utilize the results of the static phase of this program. . . ."

We look at a second opening comment to see another example of how this subarea encourages your readers to read your work by offering them some comforting language. The use of scientific terms known by many disciplines in this opening section gives your readership an appreciation of your ideas in familiar language.

The technical paper entitled, "Aramid Transverse Filament Properties and Hose Fitting Retention" provides an example of how you can use this familiar language to entice your audience to wade through a lengthy section of your trade paper or internal technical report:

> "Steel wire hose reinforcement is often made up of monofilament cord bundles lying adjacent to one another. These large bundles may sustain ferrule penetration without a great deal of loss in their tensile strength.

"Textile cord bundles are usually made up of many small filaments that are its fundamental building units. The strength of the textile cord bundle is a function of what percent of these filaments break at one time.

"Significant damage to fiber filaments during installation could lower the strength of the textile cord bundle thereby reducing its fitting retention capability. This suggests that filament damage studies must be done prior to accepting screwed-on fittings for multifilament textile reinforced hoses.

"Swaged fittings are more appropriate for textile reinforcements because they rely solely on compressional forces for fitting retention. Figure 3 offers a pictorial representation of these forces where the large arrows are swage nodes. Frictional forces between the hose and the fitting components are the principal retaining mechanism for fitting retention."

"This paper starts examining the contributions to the frictional force retaining the fitting. It assumes that the static friction equation is applicable in the analysis of the fitting retention.

"The filament is the fundamental building unit of the multifilament textile bundle, so an examination of the filament's transverse deformation with an applied stress offers some insight on fitting retention. Understanding the characteristics of this deformation helps in an appreciation of the normal force component in the friction equation governing the hose fitting retention during hose pressurization."

This paper uses terms that touch the textile industry, steel wire industry and hose industry. The intent is to start supplying the reinforcement knowledge to the hose manufacturers that allows them to replace heavy steel wire reinforcement with light weight high strength textiles. Since the paper's target audience is hose manufacturers and hose end users, you have merely supplied the new knowledge in language that they can understand.

The Quick White Paper

b) BACKGROUND

The background offers you an opportunity to tell of preliminary efforts you undertook that helped to define your premises or whatever experiments you elected to run. It is especially important in internal reports, where you are able to elaborate on joint efforts with co-workers or offer a chronology of internal efforts that led you to do this work.

You may not want to use this subarea in trade publications, but rather put this information in the Introduction section. However, the background section is very important when you are making presentations to specific customers and wish to remind everyone of work done in the past. This saves the reader from straining his or her memory and avoids numerous questions where your audience has no knowledge of past efforts. It also avoids the distractions associated with one or two persons bringing their detailed notes from previous meetings, thus making others feel insecure because they do not have comparable information.

On occasion, a background section enhances the clarity of the ideas you present in your trade publications. An example of this is seen in the following comments on the idea of textile filament transverse properties as significant in hose fitting retention:

> "An appreciation of hose coupling mechanisms and the acceptance that single filaments are the fundamental components of the multifilament hose reinforcement bundle lead to the hypothesis that the mechanical properties of the reinforcing filaments normal to their longitudinal axis influence coupling retention performance. Experiments were run to estimate these transverse mechanical properties of aramid reinforcing fibers and to develop a better understanding of the structural variables that influence them."

c) TEST OUTLINE

You want to make a test outline of how you intend to present your data, remembering that it should tell a story. If your readers recognize that you are about to present a clear narrative, they will feel comfortable following your logic to see how it unfolds. Their comfort with your story enhances the chances they will read your paper or report. There are two key aspects in this section:

i) Present your experimental test design, and

ii) Tell about any unique equipment you used to make measurements.

d) DATA

There are many different ways to present your data. You must find the system with which you are comfortable. However, you want to make certain that you are presenting sufficient data to support your case.

You want to keep in mind that data and chart portability are underpinning goals in your internal reports. You want to include an analysis of the data on charts, graphs, and tables. Tables like Figure V offer maximum portability between reports, articles, and presentations.

Good word processing software include equation editors, so you should not have any difficulty generating your equations. Therefore, you want to add that one additional calculation to make your derivations easy to follow, leaving the reader with the feeling that your work is user-friendly.

We can appreciate the importance of the added equation in the example below in which we established a relationship between the straight hanging, circular cord bundle face area and the parabolic faced bundle area when it is hung across a bar that simulates the hose inner-liner.

The Quick White Paper

$$1.38(\pi D_i^2)/4 = (2/3)W*T$$

D_i = Diameter of straight hanging cord bundle
W = Width of parabolic tension cord
T = Thickness of parabolic bundle
W = 2.6T

FIGURE V

CORD BUNDLE FACE AREA COMPARISON MEASUREMENT

DENIER	BAR SIZE (MM)	CORD TENSION (GRAMS)	AREA (MM^2)	AREA INCREASE (%)
1000	0	454	0.1337	0
1000	12.7	454	0.1736	30
1000	9.7	454	0.1888	41
1000	12.7	1816	0.1816	36
1000	9.7	1816	0.2072	55
2250	0	454	0.333	0
2250	12.7	454	0.4284	29
2250	9.7	454	0.4634	39

* SMALLEST BAR SIZE HAS GREATEST FACE AREA
* HIGHER TENSION INCREASES FACE AREA
* AVERAGE FACE AREA INCREASE ACROSS ALL BARS IS ~38%
* COMPARABLE AREA INCREASE AT CONSTANT TENSION

Report Elements Defined

$$1.38(\pi D_i^2)/4 = (2/3)(W^2/2.6)$$

Therefore we have 2.05 D_i = W.

On the other hand, *including insignificant data to impress people with the amount of work you did makes your internal reports or trade publications very uninteresting and even confusing to your audience.* You want to avoid this practice, for you can make your potential readership shun reading your entire paper or report. Audiences instinctively see it through the adage that success is inversely proportional to the thickness of the report.

e) RESULTS

The *results section provides the findings from your experiments or theoretical calculations and discusses them in detail.* You make your case for some position or insight you have, and you go about using your data to support this belief. You may also need to call upon the works of others in this section to support your belief.

An example of a short results section that highlighted the importance of transverse filament properties in high pressure hose fitting retention follows:

> ". . . At 25 degrees C, the transverse tensile modulus of the KEVLAR® fibers shows a generally increasing trend from 1.6 Gpa (232 kpsi) for the lowest crystallinity KEVLAR® 129, to 2.4 GPa (348 kpsi) for the highest crystallinity KEVLAR® 149. The modulus of PPD/POP-T commercial copolymer at 1.2 GPa (174 kpsi) is significantly lower than any of the KEVLAR® samples.
>
> "At 100 degrees C, the difference between the KEVLAR® and the PPD/POP-T copolymer is even more dramatic. Whereas the transverse modulus of the KEVLAR®

The Quick White Paper

did not change significantly, the modulus of the PPD/POP-T copolymer decreased ~25% from 1.2 GPa (174 kpsi) to 0.9 GPa (131 kpsi). This difference in response to elevated temperature between the KEVLAR® and the copolymer fiber is not surprising in view of the very low crystallinity of the PPD/POP-T copolymer compared to the KEVLAR®.

"The above results also offer an explanation to findings reported by DuPont Toray Kevlar to an experiment with high pressure hoses reinforced with either KEVLAR® 129 or PPD/POP-T commercial copolymer. The design burst pressure of these hoses is 1200 kg/cm^2 (roughly 17.4 kpsi). Figure 10 shows that the PPD/POP-T copolymer hose failed prematurely and the KEVLAR® 129 achieved the hose burst pressure goal. A blown off fitting was the premature failure mode. A similar experience has also been reported in the United States of America.

"These preliminary experiments suggest the potential importance of the transverse modulus of the yarn filaments. However, more testing is needed to insure that fitting installation problems or improper fitting selection are ruled out as a cause of these premature fitting failure findings."

CONCLUSION

There is always some confusion over the difference between the conclusion section and the summary section of the technical reports or trade articles. However, in the *conclusion section you want to state specifically what you concluded from your research effort.* It should consist of a few succinct statements that leave no doubt as to what you believe your data means or does not mean.

Let us continue our Kevlar® filament transverse modulus discussion by looking at an example of a conclusion section:

"The transverse modulus of a fiber is a measure of its ability to resist transverse deformation and also the amount of stress generated under a given deformation. In view of our current understanding of the mechanism of hose fitting

Report Elements Defined

retention, transverse modulus appears to be a fundamental fiber property that is relevant to textile reinforced high pressure hose performance. The data presented above suggest that KEVLAR® aramid fiber has superior transverse properties which will provide better hose fitting retention performance.

"These experiments represent initial efforts to relate fiber properties to hose fitting performance retention. In order to develop a more complete understanding, experiments to determine time dependent transverse properties (stress relaxation or creep) at hose operating temperatures are needed."

SUMMARY

The *summary section is a holistic look at what you reported*. In this section you touch on the salient points of your research to insure that your readers have an overall picture of what was done. This section is very important in that many potential readers may read only the abstract and summary or conclusion prior to deciding to invest time and effort in reading through your paper.

A typical summary section might read:

"Besides knitted hose burst pressure, coverage of the inner-liner and cord weight per hose length can be calculated. Inner-liner coverage assesses the interstitial opening availability for strike-through adhesion. Good strike-through adhesion prevents cover jacket delamination problems in hose use. Cord weight per hose length gives the hose designer a tool to estimate the cost of various hose reinforcement materials.

"An equation for cord gauge provides hose manufacturers of braided, spiral, and knitted hoses with a tool to better assess how well the textile reinforcement cord covers the inner-liner to prevent pinhole failures from inner-liner pull-through into the interstitial openings. This cord gauge

The Quick White Paper

estimate will be especially helpful to the spiral and knitted hose manufacturers since the compaction of adjacent reinforcement ends does not cause cord bundle deformation in the hose fabrication as is the case with braided hoses."

"A spreadsheet permits quick determination of hose burst pressure, inner-liner percent coverage, cord length, weight per hose length, and cord gauge. This allows the hose manufacturer to examine many designs to establish the optimum hose construction at the minimal cost."

BIBLIOGRAPHY

There is some concern over the issue of using footnotes and a bibliography or using endnotes alone. Since the issue that we are addressing here is the reader's ability to find the source materials we used in our trade paper or internal technical report, we opt for using only endnotes in the interest of rapid writing. Footnotes clutter up your pages with redundant information. There really is not an immediate need for this information during the course of the reader's assessment of your report.

A good word processing program generates the endnotes for you as you are including your reference sources into your paper. This feature is invaluable, for it will number your references automatically and even renumber them if you have to include a new reference source in a later revision of your report.

You can adopt standard formats for your endnotes found in many English textbooks. The important issue is to be consistent once you have selected a system to follow. Whichever system you select, it should include the name of the author or authors, the name of the publication, the name of the article or book, date of the article or edition of the book, volume number, and page numbers.

Report Elements Defined

An example of documentary endnotes follows:

1. Colin W. Evans, *Hose Technology*, Second Edition (London, Elsevier Applied Science, 1979).

2. V. V. Arkhipov et al, "Calculation For A Screwed Fitting For Rubber Hoses," *Soviet Engineering Research* 4, no. 10.

3. P. J. Lee, "Designing with Today's Hydraulic Hose," *Hydraulics & Pneumatics* (May 1988).

4. David Catterall, "Hydraulic Coupling Design Trends In Recent Years," *Fluid Power International* (April 1973).

5. S. Kawabata "Measurement of Transverse Mechanical Properties of High-performance Fibres," *J. Text. Inst.* 81, no. 4 (1990): 432–447.

6. S. L. Phoenix and J. Skelton, *Text. Res. J.* 44 (1974): 934–940.

7. J. Blackwell, R. A. Cageao, and A. Biswas, "X-ray Analysis of the Structure of HM-50 Copolyamide Fibers," *Marcomolecules* 20 (1987): 667–671.

8. S. Sakamoto (DuPont Toray Kevlar, Ltd.), Personal Communications to S.N. Miller, 1992–1993.

9. W. P. Cooper (E. I. DuPont De Nemours & Co. Inc), Personal Communication to S.N. Miller, 1993."

APPENDICES

Detailed derivations and explanations of data do not need to be in the body of your research report or trade paper. These discussions are best put in appendices where one can focus his or her efforts on a given item in a particular appendix.

However, you want to guard against merely exploiting appendices as vehicles to pad your paper, for they will merely

The Quick White Paper

detract from your work. You want to keep in mind the adage, "*When in doubt, leave it out!*" On the other hand, using your appendices to expand on the body of your report or paper will lend credibility to your findings.

EPILOGUE

There is a greater need today than ever before to pass scientific information between generations in corporations to insure their survival tomorrow. It is common knowledge in this information age that it is research that fuels tomorrow's prosperity. But corporate downsizing to improve competitiveness makes the task of sharing scientific information between corporate generations more difficult every day.

Scientists and engineers feel that they simply do not have the time to write internal technical reports or develop trade publications. In this new paradigm they must now wear many hats. Nevertheless, if you use some modern off-the-shelf writing tools and develop a good writing template, you will find that you are still able to generate technical reports, presentations, and trade publications in this new environment.

The Quick White Paper

Corporations need to see that their employees have a working knowledge of spreadsheets, word processors, and graphic programs running in either the Windows or Macintosh operating environments. This knowledge allows people to have the maximum portability of the work generated in any one program. You can simply use cut and paste techniques to generate many variations of a master report, assuming you wrote it to the highest standard of excellence.

This present work offers a system that permits rapid writing once scientists and engineers become accustomed to using it on a daily basis. Rapid writing becomes easier if one merely uses a little forethought when recording data during experiments and putting items into a research notebook. Simply adding conclusions to data once it is recorded saves hours of frustration later and reduces the need to look at reams of complex data at one time.

Developing a vision statement before attempting to write a report focuses the writing efforts. This exercise tells you what data is needed to paint the picture you have in mind and what should be discarded.

Once you have a clear vision statement, your task is merely one of filling in the items in the template entitled, "Technical Report Elements."

You should expect your writing difficulty to diminish as you move up the learning curve, writing reports until you find your own style. This is analogous to a muscle that hurts when you first start to use it, but which becomes less painful and even easier with practice. Therefore, you want to use the writing template philosophy as many times as you can until it becomes a part of you.

AUTHOR'S CLOSE UP

I retired after roughly twenty years experience in Technical Marketing at the E.I. Du Pont de Nemours & Co. Inc. During the latter portion of my Du Pont tenure the company merged the Technical Marketing and End-use Research organizations in the Industrial Textile Division of the Textile Fibers Department which offered me the added opportunity to do research projects. My love of research and the need to maintain my Technical Marketing responsibilities became the catalyst for developing techniques to write internal technical reports quickly.

One becomes very astute at developing trade presentations using someone else's data in Technical Marketing,

The Quick White Paper

but research requires you to generate this information in a usable form. Clearly Du Pont's action in merging the two groups blurred the line between research and marketing. It made great sense for Du Pont, considering that they were laden with scientists and engineers.

But if one is increasing the load on one's employees, the logical question becomes, "What work must get dropped off the sled?" The easiest thing for management to do is not to make any decisions and allow their people to do what they can accomplish and penalize them if they give the wrong priority to important tasks. Thus, the proverbial short range versus long range objectives haunt many people, especially in the present environment of corporate downsizing.

This tug-of-war can make the writing of technical reports appear to be a luxury that is tantamount to tomfoolery in the modern corporate psyche. One might even label this scenario as long term corporate suicide because valuable resources must be wasted to recreate defunct projects if the original inventors have all retired or left the company. However, without recording one's work, succeeding generations cannot learn from your findings. I am sure I have read hundreds of internal research reports during my Du Pont tenure that saved countless hours of duplicating previous efforts and, in turn, helped to shape my thinking on the task before me.

It was the need for preserving knowledge for the future health of the Du Pont Company that demanded that I look beyond the stereotyped techniques for writing technical papers. I have this great love for writing newspaper editorials, and though I had written over four hundred of them, I had always kept my newspaper columns separate from my technical work. Yet I found generating the editorials made me write something every day, thus sharpening my skills for other products. Therefore, producing trade presentations became a minor issue.

I had not examined the commonality between editorial writing and producing technical reports and trade papers. Somehow it seemed a sacrilege to mix technical writing and newspaper columns in the same thought process. I knew I was a living oxymoron; therefore, I later wondered if other people appreciated the importance of my writing newspaper editorials as a key element in my ability to generate technical papers quickly.

Nevertheless, a holistic look at technical and editorial writing suggested that there is more commonality than is initially apparent. Just consider a few points:

* You must have one main point per article.

* Your arguments must be based on facts and not fantasy.

* Enlightening others on an issue is the key reason for writing your work.

On the other side of this coin are the perceived differences that were mere mirages:

* Technical articles and presentations must be written to one's technical peers.

* Writing user-friendly material is a sign that your work is not elegant.

Once I accepted the fact that because people have always thought this way does not necessarily make it right, then I was free to reexamine things with a mind set of what does work. Certainly, if you want to write rapidly, newspaper people can teach you a lot because they must accomplish this feat on a daily basis to survive. I, therefore, feel a bit silly for not exploiting my newspaper experience sooner.

The Quick White Paper

Also, if you are an editorial writer, you must know how to think through issues quickly and convey them to a mass audience. That suggests that user-friendliness is an expectation of your job. Simply stated, the more people understand your points, the greater the potential of gaining the response you had in mind for writing them.

On the other hand, it is common to hear researchers complain that their reports merely collect dust. Complaints like this indicate that the material is either too complex for consumption by your target audience or perhaps it is simply long-winded and boring.

I decided to conduct an experiment where I wrote an internal Du Pont technical report using the mind set of an editorial writer. When my reviewer first looked at my selection of words in the body of the report, his initial reaction was one of concern. But I insisted upon following through with my test. I knew I was on the right course when, later, the technical director told me how he enjoyed reading one of my reports.

What I found was when I thought less as a research traditionalist, I generated technical papers, presentations, and reports that were both useful and efficiently produced.

As a newspaper man, word processing was just another tool to get something written quickly and accurately. I would not be afraid to use a graphics program to make a simple picture out of the complicated data I wanted to discuss. Hence, I concluded that people responsible for generating technology are often blinded to its use. You can find some technocrats that get powerful computers and have very powerful software loaded onto them, but these same people may never open the software manuals.

Today's software companies are producing products that are more and more user-friendly; thus, it is now time to seriously examine these new software packages' potential to increase productivity. What I find is that the modern word processing, graphics, and spreadsheet programs are at the stage in their evolution that they can provide a quantum step in report and presentation writing if one takes the time to truly learn these packages. Word processing, graphics, and spreadsheet programs running under Microsoft Windows or Apple MacIntosh environments also offer portability between reports and presentations. The idea of portability is one of the keys to rapid writing because you only have to write something once.

Another key that seems obvious is to write the technical report to the highest standard of excellence that will be needed for your audience. This permits one to use the data without the need of additional information sources and suggests that you can respond to requests very quickly.

And now, here are a couple of words on where I spend my time today. . . . Currently I am a Visiting Assistant Professor of Mathematics at Delaware State University and have served as Adjunct Instructor of Computer Science at Delaware Technical and Community College. I am also a consultant on textile hose failure analysis for multinational corporations.

I earned a Bachelor of Science Degree in Mathematics at Delaware State University in 1967 and a Masters of Science Degree in Physics from the University of Delaware in 1972 (thesis title: Photo-stimulated Release of Stored Charge in Multilayer Films of CdS and CdSe).

My non-DuPont work experiences are: Urban Agent at University of Delaware, National Science Foundation Developmental Fellow in the Physics Department at the University of Delaware, Departmental Assistant (Mathematics) at Delaware State University, Production Supervisor for the Chrysler Corporation, and Management Trainee for the International Playtex Corporation.

The Quick White Paper

My political experiences are: I ran for Lt. Governor of the State of Delaware in the 1996 General Election and today I am the Chairman of the Ethics Commission of the City of Wilmington, Delaware.

My nontechnical activities are: I offer marriage seminars where facets of one of the books my wife and I wrote entitled, *Wedlock . . . The Common Sense Marriage,* are discussed in detail. I also have given marital advice on national and international radio shows.

I continue to write a weekly column for newspapers across the United States where my primary areas of interest are business, politics, and human development. My articles have appeared in *Delaware Capitol Review, The News Journal* in Wilmington, Delaware, *Delaware State News, Philadelphia Daily News, Philadelphia Tribune, Philadelphia New Observer, Kansas State Globe, Charlotte Post, Baltimore Times, The Carolinian, The Tri-State Defender, The Pittsburgh Courier, The Journal & Guide, The Connection,* and others.

I have had letters-to-the-editor appear in *Business Week, Washington Report, Nation's Business, Black Enterprise, Richmond News Leader, The News Journal, Delaware State News,* and *Delaware Medical Journal.*

I have had magazine articles appear in the *Omega Psi Phi Oracle, Capitol Hill,* and the *Delaware State Chamber of Commerce Business Journal.*

Hence, if you take some cues from newspaper people you will find that technical writing remains a viable business option even in the midst of a rightsizing environment where everyone must wear many hats.

INDEX

Index

A

abstract 61-65
academic curiosity 32
accuracy 47-49, 50
accurate data 52
active voice 44
activities that are catalysts 37
adages 35
agendas 16
analysis of the data 77
analysis statements 53
analyzing your data today 53
ancillaries 49
appendices 83
assistants 51
assumptions 71
audience 16
audience's receptivity 45

B

background 76
bad results 60
basis of quick writing 15
bibliography 82
blank stares 46
brain 36
brand names 40-41
brevity 44
business assumptions 71
business rationale 32
business sense 32
business significance
      32, 62, 65, 66
busy charts 45

C

catalysts 37
CD-Rs 42

chart portability 77
charts 25, 29, 35, 45
clear message 39-40
clear mind 15
closure 55
comforting language 75
communicating 47
competitive advantage 32
computer crashing 55
conclusion 45, 81
conclusions 26, 32
confidence 53
confidential ideas and findings
      41-42
confidential information 26, 73
confidential report 65
confidential white papers 41
confidentiality 58
confusing 79
corporate downsizing 60
corporate resources 62
corporate secrets 42
cost/benefit 19, 28, 43, 65
credibility 19, 40, 55, 66, 84
cut-and-paste 31, 50

D

data 27, 77, 81
data analysis statements 53
data portability 27, 30
data summary 54
de facto lying 43
deception 60
definitive conclusions 63
digression 44
directions 30
discussion section 74
divine revelation 14, 36, 37
doubt 40, 54
downsizing 42, 60-61

Index

E

ego blindness 50, 55
embarrassment 40
emotion 16
endnotes 82
equation editors 78
external storage 42

F

fact and fantasy 18, 52
failure 38, 60
false information 43
false sense of security 41
familiar language 75
fate 14
fiction writing 55
fight off the urge to deceive 60
first basic principle of good writing 15
first draft 18
first family of charts 29
first hand observation 53
floppy disks 41-42
fog factor 17, 19, 39, 43
font 45
food for thought 51
footnotes 82
Forethought 16, 19, 47
four writing tools 25
fourth mental draft 19

G

generic names 40
global family 47
gobbledegook 43
good software 31
graphic 24, 45
graphic software 23

graphs 25
gut-wrenching 18

H

hacker 42
hard copies 41
hard disk drive 41
highest standard of excellence 47
historical approach 66
historical figures 16
holistic look 16, 54, 81
honest assessment 18
hype 45

I

I don't know 54
idea 36
immediate assessment 53
implied versus overt premises 71
in doubt 40
in-depth knowledge 55
in-depth understanding 51
industrial espionage 41
industrial spies 42, 73
insecure 43
insignificant data 79
integrity 71
intellectual honesty 61
interim notes 54
internal consumption 65
internal publication 25
internal reports 73, 77, 79
international units 46-47
introduction 32, 65, 68
introductory statement 32
irrelevant information 44

Index

K

key tools 23
know-it-all 55

L

laptop computers 42
liberal interpretation 55
liberal publications 68
librarian 66
lines 45
literature search 61
long report 38
luck 14

M

mainframe terminal 24
management review 30
margin 45
mass of confusion 53
mass understanding 17
master guide 58
me-too article 65
medium 40
mental draft number four 19
mild editing 32
minute details 32
misrepresented the facts 55
multiple issues 18

N

narrative 77
natural disaster 55
negative results 38
new directions 32
no stones unturned 38
non-confidential 65
non-decision-making individuals 47–49
non-secure personal computers 41
nonfiction arena 55

O

objectives 32, 66, 68, 73
observations 26
omnipotent 54
one central idea 45
one-line statements 32
opening comments 74
overriding emotion 39–40
overt and covert agendas 16
overt premises 71

P

pad 84
padding 38, 44
paper 45
paragraph form 32
paragraphs 44–45
password 41–42
personal computer 23
personally observe an experiment 52
picture 45
poor quality measurements 52
portability 29, 31, 48, 49, 77, 78
portable 25, 47, 58
power of the software 31
preliminary efforts 76
premises 23, 71, 73, 76
presentation 25
pretty charts 45
publishable 15

Q

quality work 37
quasi-sales mediums 40

Index

questionable data 40, 43
quick reports 50
quick writing 15

R

rationale 62
rationalization 60
readability 44
recipes 41
removable hard drives 42
remove references 30
report writing template 25, 58
reporting deception 61
research credibility 59
research paper 26
restating your objectives 60–61
results 63, 79
results statement 63
retrievable database 47
rewriting the objective 60
rough data 47
rules-of-thumb 35

S

say I don't know 55
scale your graphs vaguely 31
second draft 18
second family of charts 29
secondary agendas 39
self-analysis 19
sentences 44–45
share data 43–45
shelf life 47
short cuts 52
short reports 39
slide 26
specific recipes 31
spreadsheet 23
sterile journal 40
storehouse 33

strategic directions 41
strategic objectives 73
strategic or tactical directions 30
strategic or tactical objectives 66
subtle pressures 55
subtleties 50
success 38, 60, 79
suicide 54
summary 32, 54, 81
superior product 32
survey the literature 65

T

tables 25
tactical issues 18
technical chart 28
technical report 25, 26, 32
Technical Report Elements 57
technical report writing template 25
technicians 51, 52
technocratic-drab 42
temptation 60
test measurements 23
test outline 77
TEST PROGRAM 63
theoretical calculations 23
theoretical method 28
theoretical treatise 63
thick report 38
think 15
thinking 36, 37
third mental draft 18–20
trade publication 25, 26, 79
trade secrets 41–42
transparency 26
trying to do too much 18

Index

U

unclarified ideas 16
understanding 43-45
uninteresting 79
user-friendly 17, 20, 42-45, 78
user-unfriendly 19

V

value-in-use pricing 28
variations 33
vision 17, 37, 59
vision statement 17, 18-19,
 23, 59-61

W

waffling 63
when in doubt 84
Windows or Macintosh 31, 49
word processing 23
work request 52
working with your data 50
workstation 23
world marketplace 47
writer's block 13, 14
writer's ignorance 43-45
writer's paranoia 55
writing 36
writing gridlock 13
writing tool 53

NOTES

REMEMBER!
ONE OF THE KEYS TO SUCCESSFUL QUICK WRITING IS TO BE ORGANIZED, SO START GETTING YOUR THOUGHTS TOGETHER NOW ...

Notes

Notes

Notes

Notes

You may order
"The Quick White Paper"
online
by visiting our Website
at www.snmiller.com